SPECTRUM

Test Prep

Grade 8

Published by
Frank Schaffer Publications®

Frank Schaffer Publications®

Spectrum is an imprint of Frank Schaffer Publications.

Printed in the United States of America. All rights reserved. Except as permitted under the United States Copyright Act, no part of this publication may be reproduced or distributed in any form or by any means, or stored in a database or retrieval system, without prior written permission from the publisher, unless otherwise indicated.Frank Schaffer Publications is an imprint of School Specialty Publishing. Copyright © 2007 School Specialty Publishing.

Send all inquiries to:
Frank Schaffer Publications
8720 Orion Place
Columbus, Ohio 43240-2111

Spectrum Test Prep—grade 8

ISBN 0-7696-8628-1

4 5 6 HPS 11 10 09

Table of Contents

What's Inside? 5

English Language Arts

Standards and What They Mean 7

Reading and Comprehension
Responding to Nonfiction 9
Responding to Fiction 11
Interpreting Fables 13
Understanding Poetry 14
Using Etymologies to Determine
   Word Meanings 15
Using Context Clues to Determine
   Meaning 16
Mini-Test 1 18

Writing
Using Denotative and Connotative Terms . . 19
Using Nouns 20
Synonyms and Antonyms 21
Persuasive Writing 22
Adapting Writing for a Different Audience . . 23
Revising 24
Spelling 25
Punctuation 26
Figures of Speech 27
Mini-Test 2 28

Research
Choosing an Information Source 29
Evaluating Online Resources 30
Using Web Search Engines 31
Mini-Test 3 32

Cultural and Social Language Use
Social Roles and Language Use 33
Participating in a Literacy Community 34
Writing to Accomplish a Purpose 35
Mini-Test 4 36

How Am I Doing? 37

Final English Language Arts Test 39
Answer Sheet 42

Mathematics

Standards and What They Mean 43

Number and Operations
Exponential and Scientific Notation 44
Ratio, Proportion, and Rate 45
Squaring and Finding Roots 46
Commutative, Associative, and
   Distributive Properties 47
Analyzing Algorithms 48

Algebra
Linear and Nonlinear Functions 49
Slope and Intercept 50
Modeling and Solving Problems 52
Creating a Table of Values and Plotting
   Points for Linear Equations 53
Mini-Test 1 54

Geometry
Making and Testing Conjectures 55
Justifying Theories About Angles 56
Using Coordinate Geometry to
   Examine Geometric Shapes 57
Similar and Congruent Figures 58
Visualization, Spatial Reasoning, and
   Geometric Modeling 59

Measurement
Understanding Relationships Among
   Units of Measurement 61
Using Appropriate Units of Measurement . . 62
Solving Measurement Problems 63
Mini-Test 2 65

Data Analysis and Probability
Using Histograms 66
Mean, Median, Mode, Range, and
   Outliers 67
Developing and Evaluating Inferences
   and Predictions 68
Mutually Exclusive and Complementary
   Events 69

Process
Solving Problems 70
Using Mathematical Language 71
Applying Math to Other Areas 72
Communicating Mathematical Ideas 73
Mini-Test 3 74

How Am I Doing? 75

Final Mathematics Test 76
Answer Sheet 79

Social Studies

Standards and What They Mean **80**

Culture
    The Culture and Origins of the Australian
        Aborigine and New Zealand's
        Maori People 81
    Transmission of Cultural Values
        Through Textbooks. 82

Time, Continuity, and Change
    Changing Evaluations of Historical Events. . 83
    Interpreting Time Lines. 84

People, Places, and Environments
    Identifying Landforms and Waterways 85
    Mental Mapping. 86
    Language Distribution 87
    Mini-Test 1 . . . . **88**

Individual Development and Identity
    Theories of Identity Development 89
    Connections to Places 90

Individuals, Groups, and Institutions
    Group Identity and Social Class 91
    Tensions Between Belief Systems
        and Governments 92
    Mini-Test 2 . . . . **93**

Power, Authority, and Governance
    Changing the Constitution 94
    The Electoral College 95

Production, Distribution, and Consumption
    Minimum and Maximum Wages 96
    Labor Force and Gross Domestic Product . . 97
    The Consumer Price Index 98

Science, Technology, and Society
    Concerns About Scientific Advances 99
    Mini-Test 3 . . . . **100**

Global Connections
    Free Trade vs. Fair Trade 101

Civic Ideals and Practices
    Studying Media Reports of Public
        Issues and Events. 103
    Understanding Political Parties' Views. . . . 104
    Mini-Test 4 . . . . **105**

How Am I Doing? **106**

Final Social Studies Test **108**
    Answer Sheet. 111

Science

Standards and What They Mean **112**

Unifying Concepts and Processes
    Examining Evidence and Providing
        Explanations. 114
    Dichotomous Keys 115

Science as Inquiry
    Hypothesizing and Experimenting 116
    Mini-Test 1 . . . . **118**

Physical Science
    Exploring pH Value. 119
    Working with Pendulums 121

Life Science
    Populations, Cooperation, and
        Competition 122
    Basic Structures of Life 123
    Scientific Classification of Species 124

Earth and Space Science
    Earth's Structure and Plate Tectonics 125
    Mini-Test 2 . . . . **127**

Science and Technology
    Evaluating Technological Design 128

Science in Personal and Social Perspectives
    Risks and Benefits of Surgery. 129

History and Nature of Science
    Science vs. Non-Science. 130
    Mini-Test 3 . . . . **131**

How Am I Doing? **132**

Final Science Test **133**
    Answer Sheet. 136

Answer Key 137

What's Inside?

This workbook is designed to help you and your eighth grader understand what he or she will be expected to know on standardized tests.

Practice Pages

The workbook is divided into four sections: English Language Arts, Mathematics, Social Studies, and Science. The practice activities in this workbook provide students with practice in each of these areas. Each section has practice activities that have questions similar to those that will appear on the standardized tests. Students should use a pencil to fill in the correct answers and to complete any writing on these activities.

National Standards

Before each practice section is a list of the national standards covered by that section. These standards list the knowledge and skills that students are expected to master at each grade level. The shaded *What it means* sections will help to explain any information in the standards that might be unfamiliar.

Mini-Tests and Final Tests

When your student finishes the practice pages for specific standards, he or she can move on to a mini-test that covers the material presented on those practice activities. After an entire set of standards and accompanying practice pages are completed, your student should take the final test, which incorporates materials from all the practice pages in that section.

Final Test Answer Sheet

The final tests have a separate answer sheet that mimics the style of the answer sheets the students will use on the standardized tests. The answer sheets appear at the end of each final test.

How Am I Doing?

The *How Am I Doing?* pages are designed to help students identify areas where they are proficient and areas where they still need more practice. They will pinpoint areas where more work is needed as well as areas where your student excels. Students can keep track of each of their mini-test scores on these pages.

Answer Key

Answers to all the practice pages, mini-tests, and final tests are listed by page number and appear at the end of the book.

To find a complete listing of the national standards in each subject area, you can access the following Web sites:

The National Council of Teachers of English: www.ncte.org
National Council of Teachers of Mathematics: www.nctm.org/standards
National Council for the Social Studies: www.ncss.org/standards
National Science Teachers Association: www.nsta.org/standards

English Language Arts Standards

Standard 1 *(See pages 9–12.)*
Students read a wide range of print and nonprint texts to build an understanding of texts, of themselves, and of the cultures of the United States and the world; to acquire new information; to respond to the needs and demands of society and the workplace; and for personal fulfillment. Among these texts are fiction and nonfiction, classic and contemporary works.

Standard 2 *(See pages 13–14.)*
Students read a wide range of literature from many periods in many genres to build an understanding of the many dimensions (e.g., philosophical, ethical, aesthetic) of human experience.

Standard 3 *(See pages 15–17.)*
Students apply a wide range of strategies to comprehend, interpret, evaluate, and appreciate texts. They draw on their prior experience, their interactions with other readers and writers, their knowledge of word meaning and of other texts, their word identification strategies, and their understanding of textual features (e.g., sound-letter correspondence, sentence structure, context, graphics).

Standard 4 *(See pages 19–21.)*
Students adjust their use of spoken, written, and visual language (e.g., conventions, style, vocabulary) to communicate effectively with a variety of audiences and for different purposes.

Standard 5 *(See pages 22–24.)*
Students employ a wide range of strategies as they write and use different writing process elements appropriately to communicate with different audiences for a variety of purposes.

Standard 6 *(See pages 25–27.)*
Students apply knowledge of language structure, language conventions (e.g., spelling and punctuation), media techniques, figurative language, and genre to create, critique, and discuss print and nonprint texts.

Standard 7 *(See pages 29–30.)*
Students conduct research on issues and interests by generating ideas and questions, and by posing problems. They gather, evaluate, and synthesize data from a variety of sources (e.g., print and nonprint texts, artifacts, people) to communicate their discoveries in ways that suit their purpose and audience.

Standard 8 *(See page 31.)*
Students use a variety of technological and informational resources (e.g., libraries, databases, computer networks, video) to gather and synthesize information and to create and communicate knowledge.

Standard 9 *(See page 33.)*
Students develop an understanding of and respect for diversity in language use, patterns, and dialects across cultures, ethnic groups, geographic regions, and social roles.

English Language Arts Standards

Standard 10
Students whose first language is not English make use of their first language to develop competency in the English language arts and to develop understanding of content across the curriculum.

Standard 11 *(See page 34.)*
Students participate as knowledgeable, reflective, creative, and critical members of a variety of literacy communities.

Standard 12 *(See page 35.)*
Students use spoken, written, and visual language to accomplish their own purposes (e.g., for learning, enjoyment, persuasion, and the exchange of information).

English Language Arts

[1.0] # Responding to Nonfiction
Reading and Comprehension

DIRECTIONS: Read the passage below, and then answer the questions that follow.

> Oily rags packed tightly into a box or a silo filled with damp grain suddenly bursting into flames appear to be mysterious, for they have no apparent causes. But there is one cause of fire that many people don't understand or even think about—spontaneous combustion.
>
> All fires are caused by the heat that is given off when oxygen combines with some material. Fast oxidation gives off much heat and light very quickly and causes things to burn. Slow oxidation gives off no light and very little heat, not nearly enough to cause a fire. But when this little bit of heat is trapped, it cannot escape into the air. Instead, it builds up. As more and more oxidation occurs, more heat is trapped. As the material gets hotter, it oxidizes faster, and the faster oxidation produces even more heat. Finally, things get so hot that a fire starts. Damp or oily materials and powdery substances are the most likely things to produce spontaneous combustion because a little moisture makes them oxidize more quickly.

1. **Which of the following would be the best title for this passage?**
   - (A) Facts about Oxidation
   - (B) Fire Safety
   - (C) The Towering Inferno
   - (D) The Combustible "Mystery"

2. **Which of these is not a good way to store combustible materials?**
   - (F) Store the materials in a tightly packed box.
   - (G) Store the materials in a loosely packed box.
   - (H) Store the materials only when they are completely dry.
   - (J) Do not put a lid on the containers.

3. **Which of the following is the best description of *spontaneous combustion?***
   - (A) oxygen combining with some material
   - (B) no light and little heat given off
   - (C) materials that get so hot they explode into flames
   - (D) much heat and some light given off

4. **Based on the passage, which of the following is the best definition of *oxidation?***
   - (F) the addition of oxygen to a compound
   - (G) the evaporation of water from a substance
   - (H) the heating of a damp substance
   - (J) the addition of water to a compound

5. **Which of the following can you conclude from the passage?**
   - (A) There are no precautions you can take to prevent spontaneous combustion from occurring.
   - (B) Moisture is usually a contributing factor to spontaneous combustion.
   - (C) All fires are a result of spontaneous combustion.
   - (D) Scientists do not understand what causes spontaneous combustion.

6. **Which of these materials is least likely to produce spontaneous combustion?**
   - (F) gunpowder
   - (G) oily rags
   - (H) damp grain
   - (J) hot rocks

Name _____ Date _____

DIRECTIONS: Read the passage below, and then answer questions 7–10.

If you are learning to play the guitar, you might have reason to thank Nicholas Ravagni. Ravagni owns a patent that helps new guitar players figure out where to place their fingers. Ravagni obtained his patent when he was 11. He got the idea for his invention when he was only six. He designed a self-adhesive and color-coded strip of plastic that fits under a guitar's strings.

You can thank other young inventors for everyday products. Open your refrigerator. You can probably find leftovers wrapped in aluminum foil. Thank Charles Hall, a college student who began experimenting with a process to create a cheap and ready supply of aluminum. When you tune in to your favorite FM radio station, thank Edwin Armstrong. Just after the turn of the 20th century, Armstrong read a book about inventions. Only 15, he decided that he would become an inventor of radios. By the time he was in his early twenties, he had made discoveries that would lead to his development of the FM radio.

7. **Which of the following is a fact?**

   (A) Edwin Armstrong's inventions were more important than those of Charles Hall.

   (B) Hall and Armstrong would advise children to have faith in their own abilities.

   (C) Hall should have gotten better grades when he was in college.

   (D) Nicholas Ravagni was the youngest of these inventors to obtain his first patent.

8. **Which of the following can you conclude from the passage?**

   (F) Charles Hall experimented with refrigeration.

   (G) Edwin Armstrong lived about 100 years ago.

   (H) Nicholas Ravagni was a world-class guitar player.

   (J) Everyone has good ideas for inventions.

9. **Which of the following would be the best title for this passage?**

   (A) Learning the Guitar

   (B) How to Obtain a Patent

   (C) Young Inventors

   (D) Everyday Products

10. **Based on the passage, which of the following is the definition of a *patent*?**

   (F) a person receiving medical treatment

   (G) a special kind of guitar

   (H) the exclusive right to make or sell an invention

   (J) the legal right of artists to control the use and reproduction of their works

Name _____ Date _____

English Language Arts

Responding to Fiction
Reading and Comprehension

DIRECTIONS: Read the passage below, and then answer the questions that follow.

One Step At A Time

Tracy studied the girls ahead of her, numbers pinned to each hunter-green shirt. Tracy's was kelly-green. She bit her lip. "Don't worry about everything all at once," her grandmother always told her. "Break each problem into little steps."

How? No way was she going to be able to smile. Her back tucks had been so low yesterday that she'd landed on her knees. She'd been chanting too fast all week. One step at a time, she told herself, but her chest tightened.

The gym door opened, and a girl slipped inside. Tracy heard a faint "Go, Eagles!" What if she started before the judges gave her the signal? She shook her head. Worry about the tumbling. Impossible to break even that into separate steps. She had to get her timing right, keep her feet together, remember not to make duck hands. She moaned, stepping out of line.

"Where are you going?" the girl behind her said. "You're next."

Next? The gym door opened. The girl pushed Tracy inside. The judges sat at a table all the way across the polished gym floor. Tracy swallowed. She was going to throw up. She was going to faint. All those faces watching. All that distance to go.

She let her breath out in a long hiss, then took off. Halfway into her hurdle, she remembered that she hadn't yelled, hadn't made any hand signals. She pitched forward, then caught herself. Her heart thundered, and she couldn't move. Just go forward, she told herself. Just take the first step. On the second flip-flop, she realized she was rebounding high enough. She hurled herself through the back tuck, landing on both feet. She grinned, yelled "Go, Eagles," then ran forward. One step at a time.

---

1. What is the setting for this story?

_____

_____

2. What is the mascot of Tracy's school? What is the school color? How do you know?

_____

_____

_____

_____ ▷ GO

3. Which details from the story tell you that Tracy is nervous?

_____

_____

_____

_____

4. What does Tracy hope to accomplish? Which details from the story give you clues about what Tracy is doing?

_____

_____

_____

_____

5. How does the advice Tracy's grandmother gave her relate to the title of the story?

_____

_____

_____

_____

6. Which sentence in the story do you think is the story's climax?

_____

_____

_____

_____

7. At what point do you think Tracy lost her nervousness? Provide details to explain your answer.

_____

_____

_____

_____

STOP

English Language Arts

Interpreting Fables
Reading and Comprehension

DIRECTIONS: Read four of Aesop's fables below. A **fable** is a short moral story, often with animal characters. For each of the fables, choose the correct moral from the choices below.

Do not sorrow over what is lost forever.	Misery loves company.
United we stand, divided we fall.	Be content with what you have.
Gossips are to be seen and not heard.	Persuasion is better than force.
People are known by the company they keep.	Fools despise what they cannot get.

1. A man wished to purchase a donkey, and agreed with its owner that he should try out the animal before he bought him. He took the donkey home and put him in the straw-yard with his other donkeys, upon which the new animal left all the others and at once joined the one that was most idle and the greatest eater of them all. Seeing this, the man put a halter on him and led him back to his owner. On being asked how, in so short a time, he could have made a trial of him, he answered, "I do not need a trial; I know that he will be just the same as the one he chose for his companion."

   MORAL: _____

2. A Lion used to prowl about a field in which Four Oxen used to dwell. Many a time he tried to attack them; but whenever he came near they turned their tails to one another, so that whichever way he approached them he was met by the horns of one of them. At last, however, they began quarrelling among themselves, and each went off to pasture alone in a separate corner of the field. Then the Lion attacked them one by one and soon made an end of all four.

   MORAL: _____

3. A Fox caught in a trap escaped, but in so doing lost his tail. Thereafter, feeling his life a burden from the shame and ridicule to which he was exposed, he schemed to convince all the other Foxes that being tailless was much more attractive, thus making up for his own deprivation. He assembled a good many Foxes and publicly advised them to cut off their tails, saying that they would not only look much better without them, but that they would get rid of the weight of the brush, which was a very great inconvenience. One of them interrupting him said, "If you had not yourself lost your tail, my friend, you would not thus counsel us."

   MORAL: _____

4. The North Wind and the Sun disputed as to which was the most powerful, and agreed that he should be declared the victor who could first strip a wayfaring man of his clothes. The North Wind first tried his power and blew with all his might, but the keener his blasts, the closer the Traveler wrapped his cloak around him, until at last, resigning all hope of victory, the Wind called upon the Sun to see what he could do. The Sun suddenly shone out with all his warmth. The Traveler no sooner felt his genial rays than he took off one garment after another, and at last, fairly overcome with heat, undressed and bathed in a stream that lay in his path.

   MORAL: _____

STOP

English Language Arts

[2.0]

Understanding Poetry
Reading and Comprehension

DIRECTIONS: Read the passage and poem below. Then, answer the questions that follow.

Realism in literature is an attempt to describe human behavior and surroundings exactly as they appear in life. Realism developed in the mid-19th century in reaction to **romanticism**. Romantic poets thought feelings and the imagination were the best way to find the truth. They often focused on nature and the past and tried to express their inner feelings about life. Realistic poets, in contrast, tried to show life as it truly was and avoided sentiment or a focus on their feelings.

Ah, Are You Digging on My Grave?
by Thomas Hardy

"Ah, are you digging on my grave,
My loved one?—planting rue?"
—"No: yesterday he went to wed
One of the brightest wealth has bred.
'It cannot hurt her now,' he said,
'That I should not be true.'"

"Then who is digging on my grave,
My nearest dearest kin?"
—"Ah, no: they sit and think, 'What use!
What good will planting flowers produce?
No tendance of her mound can loose
Her spirit from Death's gin.'"

"But someone digs upon my grave?
My enemy?—prodding sly?"
—"Nay: when she heard you had
      passed the Gate
That shuts on all flesh soon or late,
She thought you no more worth her hate,
And cares not where you lie."

"Then, who is digging on my grave?
Say—since I have not guessed!"
—"O it is I, my mistress dear,
Your little dog, who still lives near,
And much I hope my movements here
Have not disturbed your rest?"

"Ah yes! You dig upon my grave . . .
Why flashed it not to me
That one true heart was left behind!
What feeling do we ever find
To equal among human kind
A dog's fidelity!"

"Mistress, I dug upon your grave
To bury a bone, in case
I should be hungry near this spot
When passing on my daily trot.
I am sorry, but I quite forgot
It was your resting place."

1. **Do you think this poem is an example of realism or romanticism? Explain your answer.**

_____

_____

2. **In the space below, write your interpretation of the poem.**

_____

_____

STOP

English Language Arts

3.0

Using Etymologies to Determine Word Meanings
Reading and Comprehension

DIRECTIONS: Etymology is the study of word origins and the history of words. Many of the words we use every day developed from words in other languages. Answer the questions below to learn about the history of English words.

1. Which of these words probably comes from the Middle English word *fæger,* meaning *lovely or pleasant?*

   (A) flower

   (B) fire

   (C) fair

   (D) flat

2. Which of these words is probably related to *arsus,* a Latin word meaning *burned?*

   (F) arsenal

   (G) arson

   (H) arrow

   (J) assumption

3. Which of these words probably comes from a German word meaning *the region behind the coast or river banks?*

   (A) kindergarten

   (B) glockenspiel

   (C) bratwurst

   (D) hinterland

4. Which of these words probably comes from a French word meaning *dark-haired?*

   (F) jolie

   (G) petite

   (H) blonde

   (J) brunette

5. Which of these words probably comes from a Spanish word meaning *table?*

   (A) valley

   (B) mesa

   (C) mountain

   (D) river

6. Which of these words is probably related to the Old Norse word *rangr,* meaning *unjust?*

   (F) wrong

   (G) range

   (H) write

   (J) right

7. The French word *faux* means _____ .

   (A) false

   (B) small

   (C) enemy

   (D) mistake

8. Which of these words probably comes from a Bantu word meaning *ghost or departed spirit?*

   (F) trickster

   (G) elf

   (H) zombie

   (J) fairy

STOP

English Language Arts

3.0

Using Context Clues to Determine Meaning
Reading and Comprehension

DIRECTIONS: Read the paragraph below. Then, choose the word that fits best in each numbered blank.

In 90-degree heat, we _____(1)_____ through the wet, steamy jungle. All the while, we were attacked by thousands of mosquitoes, whose _____(2)_____ buzzing nearly drove us mad. We hoped to reach the small campsite before it got dark. No one wanted to spend another night in the jungle. But it was so hot, and we'd been on the move all day. Our strength was _____(3)_____. None of us believed we had the _____(4)_____ to keep going. Suddenly, a flash of color came into view just ahead of us. A toucan, _____(5)_____ splendidly on the branch of a tree up ahead, reminded us all why we'd come to the jungle in the first place. We just had to find a way to save these _____(6)_____ birds. That moment _____(7)_____ the day for us. Feeling stronger, and with a renewed sense of _____(8)_____, we continued our journey.

1. (A) strolled
    (B) slogged
    (C) skipped
    (D) ambled

2. (F) deadly
    (G) melodious
    (H) soothing
    (J) persistent

3. (A) waning
    (B) expanding
    (C) chattering
    (D) developing

4. (F) intelligence
    (G) stamina
    (H) appetite
    (J) assets

5. (A) slouching
    (B) hopping
    (C) eating
    (D) posing

6. (F) magnificent
    (G) ridiculous
    (H) dim-witted
    (J) amusing

7. (A) blemished
    (B) redeemed
    (C) ruined
    (D) explained

8. (F) dread
    (G) time
    (H) purpose
    (J) direction

GO

DIRECTIONS: Read the passage below. Then, answer the questions that follow.

A group of huntsmen were camping on the Ohio River. The **foliage** swayed in the night wind, and the **argent** light of the moon ran in fleeting bars through the dim **recesses** of the forest. From the ground arose a **ruddier** glare. High and dry, fires had been built and the flames were darting and curvetting among the trees. In the **weird** light the hunters were clustered about in squads, silently stripping their prey or preparing their weapons for **the morrow**'s chase. In the background were the women, moving here and there in the dancing shadows. One was bending low over a newborn infant, and as she uttered his name in the stillness of the evening it blended with the music of the tree-tops.

"Thayendanegea!"

The name was taken from the great book of nature. It was a birth-name of the Mohawks meaning two sticks of wood bound together, a sign of strength; and the woman hoped that her tiny child might one day be a man of **valor** among the Mohawks. Could she have but known it, her desire was to be more than realized, for in **vigor** of mind and body he was destined to surpass all the **offspring** of his race.

—from *The War Chief of the Six Nations*,
by Louis Aubrey Wood

DIRECTIONS: Each of the words or phrases below is a definition for one of the **bold** words in the passage above. Write the correct word from the passage next to each definition below.

_____ 9. **more reddish**

_____ 10. **heroism**

_____ 11. **things that are set back away from other things**

_____ 12. **descendants; members of one's family tree**

_____ 13. **silvery white**

_____ 14. **the next day**

_____ 15. **leaves of plants and trees**

_____ 16. **strength, energy, health**

_____ 17. **very odd or unusual**

18. **Who are the people being described in the passage? What are they doing? Who is Thayendanegea? How does the passage give you clues about Thayendanegea's future?**

_____

_____

_____

STOP

English Language Arts

| 1.0–3.0 |

For pages 9–17

Mini-Test 1

Reading and Comprehension

DIRECTIONS: Read the passage below to answer questions 1–6.

Propaganda is the distribution of ideas and information to persuade people or to **intensify** specific attitudes and actions. Although **massive** wartime propaganda techniques began with World War I, propaganda activities escalated greatly during World War II. The Axis powers tried to weaken the **morale** of the Allied armed forces and civilian populations by radio propaganda and by dropping leaflets onto civilians and Allied troops. The Allies, in turn, attempted to separate the citizens of the Axis nations from their governments, whom they blamed **solely** for the war. Radio broadcasts and leaflets dropped from the air carried Allied propaganda to the enemy.

1. Based on the passage, you can conclude that _____ .

  (A) propaganda is rarely used today

  (B) propaganda can be used for many different reasons

  (C) only the "bad guys" use propaganda

  (D) the use of propaganda began during World War II

2. Which of the following would be the best title for this passage?

  (F) The Causes of World War II

  (G) The Evil of Nazism

  (H) Propaganda During World War II

  (J) The Deceit of the Axis

DIRECTIONS: Each of the phrases below is a definition for one of the **bold** words in the passage. Write the correct word from the passage next to each definition below.

_____ 3. huge; imposing in size

_____ 4. entirely, totally

_____ 5. to make something stronger

_____ 6. one's spirit or state of mind

DIRECTIONS: Choose the best answer.

7. Which of these words probably comes from an Italian word meaning *little strings*?

  (A) umbrella   (C) piano

  (B) confetti   (D) spaghetti

DIRECTIONS: Read the poem below, and then write your interpretation of the poem in the space that follows.

To the maiden
The sea was blue meadow,
Alive with little froth-people
Singing.

To the sailor, wrecked,
The sea was dead grey walls
Superlative in vacancy,
Upon which nevertheless at fateful time
Was written
The grim hatred of nature.
—from "War is Kind," by Stephen Crane

8. _____

_____

_____

_____

_____

_____

English Language Arts

[4.0]

Using Denotative and Connotative Terms
Writing

Example:

The model *walked* down the runway. The model *slinked* down the runway.

The word *slinked* has a different connotative meaning from *walked,* even though both have similar denotative meanings.

 Clue

Words that convey an exact, dictionary meaning are *denotative terms.* Words that carry emotional, humorous, or positive/negative associations are *connotative terms.*

DIRECTIONS: Choose the word or phrase that has the more negative connotation to complete sentences 1–3.

1. Martin had an _____ (excuse, explanation) for not turning in his homework.

2. The _____ (slim, skinny) woman grabbed her coat as she headed out the door.

3. Ingrid is _____ (enthusiastic about, obsessed with) that new singer from England.

DIRECTIONS: Choose the word or phrase that has the more positive connotation to complete sentences 4–6.

4. Brian had an _____ (innocent, immature) love of animals.

5. Her mother's perfume had a strong _____ (aroma, stench).

6. LaToya is very _____ (sensitive, thin-skinned) when she is criticized.

DIRECTIONS: On the lines below, write two paragraphs about last night's dinner. In the first paragraph, use denotative terms to tell exactly what happened. In the second paragraph, use connotative terms to make readers wish they had been there with you.

7. _____

_____

_____

_____

_____

_____

_____

_____

_____

_____

_____

_____

_____

STOP

English Language Arts

| 4.0 |

Using Nouns
Writing

DIRECTIONS: Write a proper noun for each common noun given below. Then, write a sentence using the proper noun.

1. country _____

_____

2. sports team _____

_____

3. park _____

_____

4. teacher _____

_____

5. friend _____

_____

DIRECTIONS: Change the following singular nouns to plural nouns.

6. cactus   _____

7. analysis   _____

8. wife   _____

9. criterion   _____

10. echo   _____

DIRECTIONS: Change the following plural nouns to singular nouns.

11. halves   _____

12. volcanoes   _____

13. phenomena   _____

14. nuclei   _____

15. crises   _____

DIRECTIONS: Rewrite the sentences below to make the nouns in **bold** possessive.

Example: My **son-in-law's** birthday is next week.

16. Karen was worried about her **mother and father** health.

_____

_____

17. The **letter carrier** job requires him to walk several miles each day.

_____

_____

18. Our teacher asked us to interpret the ten **poems** symbolic language.

_____

_____

STOP

Synonyms and Antonyms
Writing

DIRECTIONS: Choose the synonym of the underlined word.

1. to cherish
- Ⓐ distort
- Ⓑ fool
- Ⓒ adore
- Ⓓ loathe

2. antique vase
- Ⓕ valuable
- Ⓖ unpleasant
- Ⓗ timid
- Ⓙ old

3. an opponent
- Ⓐ colleague
- Ⓑ friend
- Ⓒ foe
- Ⓓ chum

4. something dense
- Ⓕ long
- Ⓖ outside
- Ⓗ thick
- Ⓙ mountainous

5. to commence
- Ⓐ close
- Ⓑ start
- Ⓒ fill
- Ⓓ peddle

6. to vault
- Ⓕ attempt
- Ⓖ reply
- Ⓗ answer
- Ⓙ leap

DIRECTIONS: Choose the antonym of the underlined word.

7. desolate city
- Ⓐ dry
- Ⓑ average
- Ⓒ desert
- Ⓓ crowded

8. lanky man
- Ⓕ short
- Ⓖ tall
- Ⓗ stocky
- Ⓙ thin

9. to whisper
- Ⓐ smell
- Ⓑ endure
- Ⓒ calm
- Ⓓ shout

10. to locate
- Ⓕ pinpoint
- Ⓖ collapse
- Ⓗ lose
- Ⓙ find

11. filled with sorrow
- Ⓐ joy
- Ⓑ sadness
- Ⓒ silly
- Ⓓ stoic

12. great peril
- Ⓕ danger
- Ⓖ quiet
- Ⓗ malice
- Ⓙ safety

STOP

Name _____ Date _____

5.0

Persuasive Writing
Writing

DIRECTIONS: Write a composition that either agrees or disagrees with the following statement:

Global warming is a serious problem facing the world today.

Answer the questions below to help you plan and organize your composition.

1. **What is your position on this topic?**

   _____

   _____

2. **What evidence do you have to support your position?**

   _____

   _____

   _____

3. **What sources did you use to find more information on the topic?**

   _____

   _____

   _____

4. **Find graphs, charts, or other visuals that give you information about the topic. What additional information do they provide?**

   _____

   _____

   _____

5. **What are the arguments that oppose your position? How can you address these arguments in your composition?**

   _____

   _____

   _____

6. **Now, write your persuasive composition on a separate sheet of paper. Assume that your classmates are your audience. State your position clearly and present evidence for your position. Include graphs, charts, or other visuals as part of your composition. Be sure to address any points on which your audience might disagree.**

STOP

Name _____   Date _____

5.0

Adapting Writing for a Different Audience
Writing

DIRECTIONS: Adapt (change) the composition you wrote for the activity on page 22. For your new composition, assume that your audience is a class of third-graders who have just begun to learn about global warming. Use the space below to adapt your composition for this new audience.

 You will need to change your essay so that this new audience can understand it. You will want to use simpler language and make the essay shorter.

_____

_____

_____

_____

_____

_____

_____

_____

_____

_____

_____

_____

_____

_____

_____

_____

_____

_____

_____

STOP

5.0

Revising
Writing

DIRECTIONS: Read the passage below, and then answer the questions that follow.

> **(1)** U.S. Representative David McDavid today introduced Bill 409 to the House of Representatives. **(2)** McDavid reports that Internet e-mail and instant messaging services cost the U.S. Postal Service in lost postage fees. **(3)** Bill 409 would permit the U.S. Postal Service to charge a five-cent surcharge on each e-mail sent. **(4)** McDavid has stated that he is not an avid user of the Internet. **(5)** The Internet service provider would be sent a bill by the U.S. Postal Service, and then the sender of the e-mail would be sent a bill by the Internet service provider. **(6)** Representative McDavid reports that no final decision has been made on charging for instant messaging services. **(7)** This surcharge may be added to the bill at a later time. **(8)** Attorney Ronald Sneed of Omaha, Nebraska, has agreed to fight this bill. **(9)** He has filed a class-action suit on behalf of a group of frequent Internet users. **(10)** Sneed has asked that citizens forward this e-mail to everyone on their mailing list, in order to alert citizens of this new charge.

1. How are sentences 8 and 9 best combined?

Ⓐ Attorney Ronald Sneed of Omaha, Nebraska, has filed a class-action suit on behalf of a group of frequent Internet users, and he has agreed to fight this bill.

Ⓑ Fighting the bill, attorney Ronald Sneed of Omaha, Nebraska, has filed a class-action suit on behalf of a group of frequent Internet users.

Ⓒ Attorney Ronald Sneed will fight the bill on behalf of a group of frequent Internet users from Omaha, Nebraska.

Ⓓ Attorney Ronald Sneed of Omaha, Nebraska, has agreed to fight this bill, filing a class-action suit on behalf of a group of frequent Internet users.

2. Which sentence does not belong in this passage?

Ⓕ sentence 1

Ⓖ sentence 4

Ⓗ sentence 7

Ⓙ sentence 10

3. How is sentence 5 best written?

Ⓐ The sender of the e-mail would be charged by the Internet service provider, because the Internet service provider would have been sent a bill previously by the U.S. Postal Service.

Ⓑ The U.S. Postal Service would send a bill for the five-cent surcharge to the Internet service provider, and then the Internet service provider would send a bill for the surcharge to the person who sent the e-mail.

Ⓒ The U.S. Postal Service would bill the Internet service provider, which would then charge the sender of the e-mail.

Ⓓ The Internet service provider would be sent a bill by the U.S. Postal Service; the service provider would therefore charge the sender of the e-mail.

English Language Arts

6.0

Spelling
Writing

DIRECTIONS: For each group of words below, choose the word that is spelled incorrectly.

1. (A) admirable
   (B) advertise
   (C) agreeable
   (D) alledge

2. (F) besiege
   (G) bookkeeper
   (H) brief
   (J) brocolli

3. (A) caffeine
   (B) colaborate
   (C) colossal
   (D) commitment

4. (F) eligible
   (G) energy
   (H) embarassed
   (J) enforceable

5. (A) hemorage
   (B) heresy
   (C) hierarchy
   (D) hypocrisy

6. (F) livable
   (G) lonliness
   (H) manageable
   (J) maneuver

7. (A) misspelling
   (B) misstate
   (C) movable
   (D) necesary

8. (F) omitted
   (G) omnicient
   (H) oppressive
   (J) orator

9. (A) parallel
   (B) passable
   (C) passtime
   (D) perceive

10. (F) presumptuous
    (G) priviledge
    (H) proceed
    (J) profited

11. (A) satelite
    (B) secession
    (C) seizure
    (D) sensitive

12. (F) suddenness
    (G) sufficient
    (H) superintendant
    (J) supersede

STOP

English Language Arts

| 6.0 |

Punctuation
Writing

DIRECTIONS: For each group of sentences below, choose the sentence that is punctuated incorrectly. If all sentences in a group are correct, choose "all are correct."

1. (A) She said the same thing over and over: Those who forget the past are doomed to repeat it.

   (B) Marlena said she always tried to, "go with the flow."

   (C) "Have you heard the story of Paul Revere?" asked Randall.

   (D) all are correct

2. (F) Her tape collection includes several folk singers (eg Pete Seeger).

   (G) Kanye said, "My favorite song is Johnny Cash's 'I Walk the Line.'"

   (H) The princess herself could not have been more radiant.

   (J) all are correct

3. (A) Miriam is a great Sudoku player; her brain is like a computer.

   (B) Before the movie began, we had to sit through a lot of long, boring trailers.

   (C) This job is quite demanding, nevertheless, I appreciate the opportunity to gain experience.

   (D) all are correct

4. (F) Alan waved good-bye to Mr. Tipton; Esther; and his brother Phillip.

   (G) My father quit his factory job and never regretted it for a moment.

   (H) Peggy asked, "Will you be going to the party with us tomorrow, Mikayla?"

   (J) all are correct

5. (A) We will arrive in Chicago by 11 o'clock because we will take a shortcut.

   (B) Did Robert really say that he believes scrubbing floors is "women's work"?

   (C) My sister always asks, "When can I get my driver's license?"

   (D) all are correct

6. (F) My friend Laura, who is an artist, displays paintings in every room of her house.

   (G) Have you ever heard the word "eradicate"?

   (H) Aside from Elvis Presley who has had the most influence on rock music?

   (J) all are correct

7. (A) The television show "Veronica Mars" is one of my favorites.

   (B) My pockets are empty; it's time to visit the ATM machine.

   (C) Central High is known for providing its students with a well-rounded education.

   (D) all are correct

8. (F) Ernest Hemingway wrote "A Farewell to Arms;" he also wrote "The Sun Also Rises."

   (G) "Do you know where we are, Tim?" asked Julie.

   (H) My neighbor's dog, Chomps, has a bite much worse than his bark.

   (J) all are correct

STOP

English Language Arts

6.0

Figures of Speech
Writing

Clue

Hyperbole occurs when you exaggerate a point that you are trying to make.
Understatement is the opposite of hyperbole; it implies more than is actually stated.
A **pun** is a play on words that is used to remind the reader of another word or words.
A **simile** is a comparison between two dissimilar objects, using *as* or *like* to connect the objects.
A **metaphor** is similar to a simile, except that a metaphor compares two dissimilar objects without using *as* or *like*.
Personification represents an inanimate object, animal, or abstraction as having human qualities and characteristics.

DIRECTIONS: For each sentence below, identify the figure of speech being used.

1. Bruno is the anchor of the Giants' offensive line. _____

2. Billy is so hungry he could eat a horse. _____

3. Jenifer doesn't relish the thought of putting ketchup on her hot dog. _____

4. It hurt a little bit when I broke my arm. _____

5. I did okay on my math test; I got a grade of 100. _____

6. When Carolyn is angry, she's like a hurricane. _____

7. My little sister is an angel. _____

8. Shrieking wildly, the angry wind lashed at me as I staggered home. _____

9. This fried chicken tastes absolutely fowl. _____

10. Rebecca was happy as a flag waving on the 4th of July. _____

11. The tree jumped into the road right in front of my car. _____

12. The clouds are like balls of cotton candy. _____

13. This book weighs a ton. _____

14. The Rocky Mountains are kind of big. _____

DIRECTIONS: Use figures of speech to answer questions 15 and 16.

15. Use hyperbole to tell how you felt the last time you were angry.

_____

16. Use a simile or metaphor to describe your best friend.

_____

STOP

English Language Arts

| 4.0–6.0 |

For pages 19–27

Mini-Test 2

Writing

DIRECTIONS: Question 1 shows singular and plural forms of common nouns. Choose the incorrect pair.

1.
   - (A) louse/lice
   - (B) veto/vetos
   - (C) thief/thieves
   - (D) sheep/sheep

DIRECTIONS: Choose the word that is the synonym of the underlined word.

2. to <u>respond</u>
   - (F) answer
   - (G) flex
   - (H) correspond
   - (J) dispute

DIRECTIONS: Choose the word that is the antonym of the underlined word.

3. <u>peaceful</u> country
   - (A) cowardly
   - (B) beautiful
   - (C) suspicious
   - (D) belligerent

DIRECTIONS: Identify the figure of speech being used.

4. **"This biscuit is a rock," he complained.**
   - (F) personification
   - (G) pun
   - (H) simile
   - (J) metaphor

DIRECTIONS: Choose the best answer.

5. **Which of the following words is spelled incorrectly?**
   - (A) deficient
   - (B) demagogue
   - (C) desirable
   - (D) deterance

6. **Which of the following sentences is punctuated incorrectly?**
   - (F) The policeman said "I can't figure out who stole the bike".
   - (G) A fat, grey mouse crawled along the baseboard.
   - (H) Cincinnati, Ohio, is often called *The Queen City of the West.*
   - (J) John took his daughter's temperature and made her some chicken soup.

7. **Which of the following sentences is best written?**
   - (A) Having just finished work on the cabin, the contractor stepped back, filled with pride, and admired it.
   - (B) Filled with pride, the contractor stepped back and admired the cabin he had just built.
   - (C) The contractor was filled with pride, stepping back to admire the cabin he had just built.
   - (D) The cabin he had just built filled the contractor with pride, so he stepped back and admired it.

8. **Which of the following has the most negative connotation?**
   - (F) an assertive salesman
   - (G) a forceful salesman
   - (H) a pushy salesman
   - (J) a persistent salesman

STOP

Name _____ Date _____

7.0

Choosing an Information Source
Research

DIRECTIONS: When you are gathering information for a research project, you may find that one source is better than another, depending on your needs. For each research need below, tell if a book, encyclopedia article, or periodical (magazine or newspaper) would be the best resource to use.

1. **Luther needs in-depth coverage on a very specific topic.** _____

2. **Jillian seeks an answer to a specific factual question.** _____

3. **Ramon wants information that is arranged logically, with an index and a table of contents to help guide his research.** _____

4. **Midori is looking for local news and information.** _____

5. **Alyssa wants a short general overview of her topic to scan for background information.**

   _____

6. **Noah is writing a paper on an important current event.** _____

7. **Katrina needs information written by specialists who have done extensive research.**

   _____

8. **Sammy needs the most current information on his topic.** _____

DIRECTIONS: Choose the best answer.

9. **Halle is writing a report about this year's mayor's race in Chicago. Which of these sources would give her the best information?**
   - (A) an encyclopedia article about the history of Chicago
   - (B) a biography of Richard Daley, former mayor of Chicago
   - (C) a local talk radio show that focuses on politics
   - (D) recent copies of *The Chicago Tribune*

10. **William is writing a report about the origins of the Declaration of Independence. Which of these sources would give him the best information?**
    - (F) a *Newsweek* article about Fourth of July celebrations across the nation
    - (G) a book that analyzes the political views of Thomas Jefferson
    - (H) his sister's fourth-grade history book
    - (J) an Internet discussion group called "Fans of the American Revolution"

STOP

English Language Arts

| 7.0 |

Evaluating
Online Resources
Research

DIRECTIONS: Use the Internet to find an online information source on a topic of your choice. Then, answer the questions below.

1. **What is your topic?** _____

2. **What is the address of the Web site you are reviewing?** _____

3. **What is the name of the site?** _____

4. **Was the information on the site useful or interesting? Why or why not?**

   _____

   _____

5. **Could you have gotten more information from a print source? Explain.**

   _____

   _____

6. **Does the site contain any links to other relevant sources?**

   _____

7. **How reliable is the information on the site? Consider the following:**
   - **Who is the author of this Web site? What are the author's credentials?**
   - **When was the page last updated? How do you know?**
   - **Is the information on the page current? Is it accurate? How can you find out?**

   _____

   _____

   _____

   _____

8. **Summarize your overall opinion of the content on this Web site. Would it be a good source for a research project on the topic? Why or why not?**

   _____

   _____

   _____

STOP

English Language Arts

| 8.0 |

Using Web
Search Engines
Research

DIRECTIONS: Spend some time exploring different Web search engines. In the table below, four popular search engines are listed; find a fifth one of your choice. As you use the search engines, evaluate them by completing the table below.

	AskForKids	**Google**	**MSN Search**	**Yahoo**	
Helpful search options					
Relevance ranking*					
Ease of use					
Help files					
Good points					
Bad points					
Overall rating (A = excellent; F = terrible)					

*In other words: How does the search engine decide which sites to list and in what order?

STOP

Name _____   Date _____

Mini-Test 3

Research

DIRECTIONS: Choose the best answer.

1. **Ariel is writing a report about the differences between realistic and romantic poetry. Which of these sources would give her the best information?**

   (A) encyclopedia articles on realistic and romantic poetry

   (B) the posts in an Internet discussion group on modern poetry

   (C) a biography of John Keats, a famous romantic poet

   (D) poetry reviews in *The New York Times*

2. **Zach is writing a report about the childhood and teenage years of former president Bill Clinton. Which of these sources would give him the *best* information?**

   (F) a *Time* magazine article about Clinton's life and presidency

   (G) *Selected Speeches of President Clinton*

   (H) a newspaper editorial about the effectiveness of Clinton's presidency

   (J) *My Life*, Bill Clinton's autobiography

3. **You are doing some research on space travel. You have found an interesting Web page on the topic and you are thinking about including some of the author's conclusions in your report. Which of the following should make you think twice before including the information?**

   (A) The Web page was last updated six months ago.

   (B) The author is a former astronaut.

   (C) You haven't found any other experts who make the same conclusions.

   (D) The author presents evidence for his conclusions.

DIRECTIONS: Study the table of contents below. Use it to answer question 4.

Contents/Features

27 Special Sections
Datebook
Monthly calendar of events in the southwestern states by Jan Renard.
64 Fashionably on Course
Hit the links in style with a new look from one of the top golf outfitters.
88 Fourth Avenue Street Fair
Ben Swift points out the food fare available and reviews many of the wares of the street vendors, as well as the entertainment that will be available.
92 Business
Who's New/What's New? Catch-up column about new faces and places along with info on new products and services.

103 Departments
Out & About
A round-up of some of the area's best places to visit.
120 Spotlight
Previews of several of the month's major events by Barry Long.
122 Destination Resorts
Executive editor Scott Hammond takes us to many of the more popular resorts in the Great Southwest, highlighting the amenities of each.
131 Dining Guide
Listing of the most popular restaurants in the Southwest, as well as descriptions of the signature dinners served by each.

---

4. **This magazine would be a good source for all of the following except _____ .**

   (F) how to find the most popular restaurants in the Southwest

   (G) what special events are taking place this month in the southwestern states

   (H) what's new in golf apparel

   (J) environmental problems in the Southwest

5. **Which Web search engine do you think is best for research? Explain your answer.**

   _____

   _____

   _____

   _____

English Language Arts

| 9.0 |

Social Roles and Language Use

Cultural and Social Language Use

DIRECTIONS: People have created dozens of different abbreviations to make online communications, such as e-mail and instant messaging, more efficient. The table below lists a few of these abbreviations. For each one, write the meaning of the abbreviation. Then, write a few of your own abbreviations and their meanings in the remaining spaces.

LOL	laugh out loud
TOY	1.
FYI	2.
BCNU	3.
AFAIK	4.
BTW	5.
IMHO	6.
7.	
8.	
9.	

DIRECTIONS: Suppose that you missed school yesterday because you were sick. In the spaces below, write an e-mail to a friend from English class to find out what happened and what make-up assignments you need to complete. Then, write an e-mail to your English teacher for the same reason.

 Clue — The audience and the purpose of your writing affects the words you use. You would probably use one kind of tone and vocabulary in an e-mail message to a friend and a very different one in an e-mail message to a teacher.

10. E-mail message to a friend:

11. E-mail message to a teacher:

 STOP

English Language Arts

11.0

Participating in a Literacy Community
Cultural and Social Language Use

DIRECTIONS: Read the passage below, and then answer the questions that follow.

The ancient Japanese samurai lived by a code of conduct called *Bushido*, which means *the way of the warrior*. Samurai fought for nobles and had to be loyal to them. They were also expected to be brave and selfless. Samurai would rather die in battle than be disloyal. They also preferred death to capture, because capture was considered a disgrace.

Bushido was influenced by a variety of religions. Shintoism helped instill in the samurai great loyalty and love of country. It taught the samurai an extreme devotion and reverence for the land of Japan and its rulers. Confucianism also influenced the samurai. It emphasized loyalty, devotion, purity, and selflessness. The samurai deeply admired Confucianism's emphasis on the moral relations between master and servant, father and son, husband and wife, older and younger brother, and friend and friend.

Buddhism's teachings about reincarnation helped the samurai be brave, even when facing death. Followers of Zen Buddhism, an important Buddhist sect, learned to control their bodies through martial arts, or sports involving combat and self-defense. This appealed to the samurai, who trained to fight without fear.

1. **How do you think American society might be different if it followed Bushido? Do you think this would be good or bad? Explain.**

   _____
   _____
   _____
   _____

2. **Many sources influenced the development of Bushido. Describe some of the things that have influenced the development of your own personal code of conduct.**

   _____
   _____
   _____
   _____

3. **Now, form a group with several classmates and share your responses to questions 1 and 2. Make sure everyone has a chance to participate. Then, name at least one thing you learned by listening to the responses of the others in your group.**

   _____
   _____
   _____
   _____
   _____

STOP

English Language Arts

| 12.0 |

Writing to
Accomplish a Purpose
Cultural and Social Language Use

DIRECTIONS: Think of the most delicious food you can imagine. Then, on the lines below, describe this food so that the reader will believe you think it tastes terrible. Do not say anything that is untrue, however.

_____

_____

_____

_____

_____

_____

_____

_____

_____

_____

_____

_____

_____

_____

_____

_____

_____

_____

_____

_____

_____

_____

_____

_____

_____

_____

STOP

English Language Arts

| 9.0–12.0 |

For pages 33–35

Mini-Test 4

Cultural and Social Language Use

DIRECTIONS: Read the letter below, and then answer the questions that follow.

Dear Governor:

I'm writing to you because I think the minimum age for getting a driver's license in our state is too high. Why do we have to be 16 before we can get a license? We can't even get a driver's permit until we are 15 1/2!!! FYI—Kids are just as able to drive as adults. They just need the chance to learn!

1. **What is the purpose of the letter?**

   (A) to entertain

   (B) to persuade

   (C) to inform

   (D) none of the above

2. **Do you think the tone and language in this letter is appropriate for its purpose? Explain your answer.**

   _____

   _____

   _____

   _____

3. **How could the writer make the letter more effective?**

   _____

   _____

   _____

   _____

   _____

   _____

DIRECTIONS: Suppose that the elected officials in your community are thinking of passing a curfew law that states that all residents under the age of 16 must be off the streets by 8:00 p.m. unless accompanied by a parent. In the space below, write an e-mail to a friend expressing your views on the subject. Then, write a letter to your elected officials for the same reason. Use a separate sheet of paper, if necessary.

4. _____

   _____

   _____

   _____

   _____

   _____

   _____

   _____

   _____

   _____

   _____

   _____

   _____

   _____

   _____

   _____

   _____

   _____

How Am I Doing?

Mini-Test 1 Page 18 **Number Correct**	**8** answers correct	**Great Job!** Move on to the section test on page 39.
	5–7 answers correct	**You're almost there!** But you still need a little practice. Review practice pages 9–17 before moving on to the section test on page 39.
	0–4 answers correct	**Oops!** Time to review what you have learned and try again. Review the practice section on pages 9–17. Then, retake the test on page 18. Now, move on to the section test on page 39.
Mini-Test 2 Page 28 **Number Correct**	**8** answers correct	**Awesome!** Move on to the section test on page 39.
	5–7 answers correct	**You're almost there!** But you still need a little practice. Review practice pages 19–27 before moving on to the section test on page 39.
	0–4 answers correct	**Oops!** Time to review what you have learned and try again. Review the practice section on pages 19–27. Then, retake the test on page 28. Now, move on to the section test on page 39.
Mini-Test 3 Page 32 **Number Correct**	**5** answers correct	**Great Job!** Move on to the section test on page 39.
	4 answers correct	**You're almost there!** But you still need a little practice. Review practice pages 29–31 before moving on to the section test on page 39.
	0–3 answers correct	**Oops!** Time to review what you have learned and try again. Review the practice section on pages 29–31. Then, retake the test on page 32. Now, move on to the section test on page 39.

How Am I Doing?

Mini-Test 4	4 answers correct	**Terrific!** Move on to the section test on page 39.
Page 36 **Number Correct**	3 answers correct	**You're almost there!** But you still need a little practice. Review practice pages 33–35 before moving on to the section test on page 39.
	0–2 answers correct	**Oops!** Time to review what you have learned and try again. Review the practice section on pages 33–35. Then, retake the test on page 36. Now, move on to the section test on page 39.

Final English Language Arts Test
for pages 9–35

DIRECTIONS: Read the passage below and then answer questions 1–4.

Matthew Brady opened his first photography studio in 1844. The images produced were daguerreotypes, recorded images on sheets of copper, coated with silver. They required long exposures to produce the image. A person being photographed would have to stay perfectly still for three to fifteen minutes. That made daguerreotypes impractical for portraits. By 1855, though, Brady was advertising a new type of image that had just been invented: a photograph made on paper.

From the beginning of his career, Brady thought that photography could serve an important purpose. His images could create a record of national life. When the Civil War broke out, he wanted to document the war. Although his costs were prohibitive and his friends discouraged him, he assembled a corps of photographers. He also bought photographs from others returning from the field. His efforts culminated in an 1862 display of photographs made after the Battle of Antietam. The bloodshed shocked the exhibit's visitors, most of whom had never known what warfare was like.

His goal was to use powerful photos to end all war. Brady did not stop warfare, of course. He did not even earn enough money to pay for his venture. Still, Brady recorded one of the most important episodes in American history. In doing so, he created the first photodocumentation of a war.

1. **The main idea of this passage is _____ .**

   (A) Matthew Brady's new type of photography

   (B) the bloodshed of the Civil War

   (C) Mathew Brady's use of photography to document the Civil War

   (D) portrait photography in the 1800s

2. **The new technology that helped Brady to photograph real life was _____ .**

   (F) the daguerreotype

   (G) photographs made on paper

   (H) digital images

   (J) the camera

3. **Daguerreotypes are images recorded on _____ .**

   (A) coated paper

   (B) copper sheets

   (C) silver nitrate

   (D) plaster

4. **Brady wanted his photos to _____ .**

   (F) create a record of national life

   (G) create a pathway for young photographers

   (H) help him get rich

   (J) set a standard for excellence in portrait photography

DIRECTIONS: Choose the best answer.

5. **Which of the following English words is related to the Spanish word *cargar,* or *to load?***

   (A) caramel

   (B) cargo

   (C) carnival

   (D) carpet

GO

6. **Which of the following is an antonym for the word *enmity*?**

   - (F) friendship
   - (G) hatred
   - (H) disappointment
   - (J) relief

7. **The plural of *fungus* is _____ .**

   - (A) fungus
   - (B) fungi
   - (C) fungae
   - (D) fungus's

8. **Which of the following is an example of a pun?**

   - (F) I think of you a million times a day.
   - (G) Seven days without laughter makes one weak.
   - (H) My sister has a mind like a computer.
   - (J) My dad is so tall, Sir Edmund Hillary tried to climb him!

9. **Which of the following would probably be the best source of information about an upcoming presidential election?**

   - (A) a recent article in a news magazine
   - (B) an encyclopedia article about presidential elections
   - (C) a book about famous American presidents
   - (D) a Web site that was last updated two years ago

10. **In what type of communication would it be most appropriate to use abbreviations like "LOL" and "BTW"?**

    - (F) an e-mail to a friend
    - (G) a letter to the editor
    - (H) a cover letter for a resume
    - (J) a letter to your grandmother

11. **Which of the following has the most negative connotation?**

    - (A) frugal
    - (B) thrifty
    - (C) cost-conscious
    - (D) stingy

12. **Which of the following sentences contains incorrect punctuation?**

    - (F) Grandfather raked the leaves; later, he dumped them into the compost pile.
    - (G) The following animals are mammals: dogs, cats, and hamsters.
    - (H) The fast-moving rabbit escaped the hungry fox.
    - (J) Tina never worried, about the weather.

13. **Which of the following words is spelled incorrectly?**

    - (A) professional
    - (B) autograf
    - (C) authentic
    - (D) athlete

DIRECTIONS: For questions 14–15, choose the word that best completes each blank.

14. **Mia's family was most impressed with the _____ setting of the cabin in the forest.**

    - (F) tranquil
    - (G) warlike
    - (H) everyday
    - (J) expensive

15. **Because the knife was dull, I had to _____ the blade.**

    - (A) burn
    - (B) carry
    - (C) sharpen
    - (D) roll

GO

DIRECTIONS: Read the poem below, and then answer questions 16–19.

I bring fresh showers for the thirsting flowers,
From the seas and the streams;
I bear light shade for the leaves when laid
In their noonday dreams.
From my wings are shaken the dews that waken
The sweet buds every one,
When rocked to rest on their mother's breast,
As she dances about the sun.
I wield the flail of the lashing hail,
And whiten the green plains under,
And then again I dissolve it in rain,
And laugh as I pass in thunder.

—*from* "The Cloud,"
by Percy Bysshe Shelley

16. **Which of the following is a clue that Shelley is considered a romantic poet?**

Ⓕ   The poem focuses on nature.

Ⓖ   The poem describes life as it actually occurs.

Ⓗ   The poem is unsentimental.

Ⓙ   All poets who wrote in the early 1800s were romantic poets.

17. **In this poem, a synonym for the word *bear* would be _____ .**

Ⓐ   tolerate

Ⓑ   bring

Ⓒ   endure

Ⓓ   destroy

18. **In this poem, the word *wield* means _____ .**

Ⓕ   to cast a spell on

Ⓖ   to laugh about

Ⓗ   to forget

Ⓙ   to use or control

19. **Which figure of speech is present in this poem?**

Ⓐ   irony

Ⓑ   hyperbole

Ⓒ   personification

Ⓓ   understatement

DIRECTIONS: Read the paragraph below, and then answer questions 20–21.

(1) One of the most fascinating figures on ancient artifacts is that of Kokopelli. **(2)** Kokopelli is compelling, not only because he is cute and vibrant, but because he is everywhere. **(3)** Several Native American tribes, including the Hopi, Zuni, Winnebago, and Anasazi, tell stories and depict images of the flute playing, hunch-backed little man. **(4)** Each tribe's idea of just who Kokopelli was is a little different. **(5)** Kokopelli T-shirts are very popular in the Southwest.

20. **Which sentence should be left out of this paragraph?**

Ⓕ   sentence 1

Ⓖ   sentence 2

Ⓗ   sentence 4

Ⓙ   sentence 5

21. **Choose the best opening sentence to add to this paragraph.**

Ⓐ   Native Americans loved Kokopelli because he played a flute.

Ⓑ   Native Americans chronicled their lives and their myths through the ancient inscriptions and pictographs found on the artifacts of their culture.

Ⓒ   Images of Kokopelli are found on jewelry, key chains, and T-shirts all over the Southwest.

Ⓓ   Southwestern Native Americans worshipped characters like Kokopelli because they loved his music.

Name _____ Date _____

Final English Language Arts Test
Answer Sheet

1 Ⓐ Ⓑ Ⓒ Ⓓ
2 Ⓕ Ⓖ Ⓗ Ⓙ
3 Ⓐ Ⓑ Ⓒ Ⓓ
4 Ⓕ Ⓖ Ⓗ Ⓙ
5 Ⓐ Ⓑ Ⓒ Ⓓ
6 Ⓕ Ⓖ Ⓗ Ⓙ
7 Ⓐ Ⓑ Ⓒ Ⓓ
8 Ⓕ Ⓖ Ⓗ Ⓙ
9 Ⓐ Ⓑ Ⓒ Ⓓ
10 Ⓕ Ⓖ Ⓗ Ⓙ

11 Ⓐ Ⓑ Ⓒ Ⓓ
12 Ⓕ Ⓖ Ⓗ Ⓙ
13 Ⓐ Ⓑ Ⓒ Ⓓ
14 Ⓕ Ⓖ Ⓗ Ⓙ
15 Ⓐ Ⓑ Ⓒ Ⓓ
16 Ⓕ Ⓖ Ⓗ Ⓙ
17 Ⓐ Ⓑ Ⓒ Ⓓ
18 Ⓕ Ⓖ Ⓗ Ⓙ
19 Ⓐ Ⓑ Ⓒ Ⓓ
20 Ⓕ Ⓖ Ⓗ Ⓙ

21 Ⓐ Ⓑ Ⓒ Ⓓ

Mathematics Standards

Standard 1—Number and Operations *(See pages 44–48.)*
  A. Understand numbers, ways of representing numbers, relationships among numbers, and number systems.
  B. Understand meanings of operations and how they relate to one another.
  C. Compute fluently and make reasonable estimates.

Standard 2—Algebra *(See pages 49–53.)*
  A. Understand patterns, relations, and functions.
  B. Represent and analyze mathematical situations and structures using algebraic symbols.
  C. Use mathematical models to represent and understand quantitative relationships.
  D. Analyze change in various contexts.

Standard 3—Geometry *(See pages 55–60.)*
  A. Analyze characteristics and properties of two- and three-dimensional shapes and develop mathematical arguments about geometric relationships.
  B. Specify locations and describe spatial relationships using coordinate geometry and other representational systems.
  C. Apply transformations and use symmetry to analyze mathematical situations.
  D. Use visualization, spatial reasoning, and geometric modeling to solve problems.

Standard 4—Measurement *(See pages 61–64.)*
  A. Understand measurable attributes of objects and the units, systems, and processes of measurement.
  B. Apply appropriate techniques, tools, and formulas to determine measurement.

Standard 5—Data Analysis and Probability *(See pages 66–69.)*
  A. Formulate questions that can be addressed with data and collect, organize, and display relevant data to answer them.
  B. Select and use appropriate statistical methods to analyze data.
  C. Develop and evaluate inferences and predictions that are based on data.
  D. Understand and apply basic concepts of probability.

Standard 6—Process *(See pages 70–73.)*
  A. Problem Solving
  B. Reasoning and Proof
  C. Communication
  D. Connections
  E. Representation

Mathematics

| 1.A |

Exponential and Scientific Notation

Number and Operations

DIRECTIONS: Multiples of 10 have special meaning in our number system. Find the value of the exponential expressions below.

1. $10^1 =$

2. $10^2 =$

3. $10^3 =$

4. $10^4 =$

5. $10^5 =$

6. $10^6 =$

7. **What is the relationship between the value of the exponent and the number of zeros in your answer?**

_____

_____

_____

DIRECTIONS: Find the decimal value for each of the following exponential expressions.

> **Example:**
>
> Multiplying or dividing by multiples of 10 moves the decimal point in a number. Mathematicians and scientists use exponents as shorthand for writing these operations. Multiplying means moving the decimal to the right. The 4 in the exponent tells us to move the decimal 4 places.
>
> 8.32×10^4
> $8.32 \times 10^4 = 8.32 \times 10,000$
>
> $8.32 = 83,200$

8. $2.4569 \times 10^3 =$

9. $5.9 \times 10^2 =$

10. $6.15892 \times 10^5 =$

11. $2.34 \times 10^1 =$

12. $6.8 \times 10^4 =$

13. $5.3498 \times 10^6 =$

14. $76.4 \times 10^2 =$

15. $18.39426 \times 10^5 =$

16. $73.215 \times 10^3 =$

STOP

Name _____   Date _____

Ratio, Proportion, and Rate
Number and Operations

Clue A **ratio** is a comparison of two numbers. A **proportion** is an equation with a ratio on each side. Proportions state that two ratios are equal. A **rate** is a ratio that expresses how long it takes to do something.

DIRECTIONS: Ivy's backpack contains 3 CDs, 4 cassette tapes, 7 books, and 1 cell phone. Use this information to answer questions 1 and 2.

1. **What is the ratio of books to cassette tapes in Ivy's backpack?**
   - (A) 7:15
   - (B) 7:4
   - (C) 15:7
   - (D) 4:7

2. **What is the ratio of CDs to the total number of items in the backpack?**
   - (F) 16:4
   - (G) 15:3
   - (H) 4:16
   - (J) 3:15

DIRECTIONS: Choose the best answer.

3. **Which of the following ratios are equal?**
   - (A) 4 to 3 and 6:8
   - (B) 3 to 4 and 8:6
   - (C) 3 to 4 and 6:8
   - (D) All of the above ratios are equal.

4. **Which of the following ratios is equal to 7:14?**
   - (F) 20 to 10
   - (G) 31 to 62
   - (H) 17 to 40
   - (J) 4 to 3

5. **24:40 =**
   - (A) 3:5
   - (B) 2:4
   - (C) 12:10
   - (D) 1:2

6. **A:B = 2:5 and A = 6. Find B.**
   - (F) 5
   - (G) 12
   - (H) 15
   - (J) 30

DIRECTIONS: Salvador ran 4 laps in 30 minutes. Use this information to answer questions 7–9.

7. **Which of the following expresses the ratio of laps to minutes?**
   - (A) 1:7
   - (B) 30:4
   - (C) 2:15
   - (D) all of the above

8. **At the rate Salvador is running, how far could he run in 45 minutes?**
   - (F) 5 laps
   - (G) 6 laps
   - (H) 8 laps
   - (J) 9 laps

9. **At the rate Salvador is running, how many hours will it take him to run 1 lap?**
   - (A) $\frac{1}{8}$ hour
   - (B) $\frac{1}{4}$ hour
   - (C) $\frac{1}{2}$ hour
   - (D) 1 hour

STOP

Mathematics

1.B

Squaring and Finding Roots
Number and Operations

DIRECTIONS: Choose the best answer.

1. **The square root of 31 is between which two whole numbers?**
   - (A) 4 and 5
   - (B) 5 and 6
   - (C) 6 and 7
   - (D) 7 and 8

2. **The square root of 53 is between which two whole numbers?**
   - (F) 4 and 5
   - (G) 5 and 6
   - (H) 6 and 7
   - (J) 7 and 8

3. **The square root of 60 is closest to**
   - (A) 7.05
   - (B) 7.25
   - (C) 7.75
   - (D) 7.95

4. **The square root of 105 is closest to**
   - (F) 9.25
   - (G) 10.25
   - (H) 11.25
   - (J) 12.25

5. **5 is the square root of**
   - (A) 10
   - (B) 15
   - (C) 25
   - (D) 100

6. $\sqrt{9} =$
   - (F) 90
   - (G) 81
   - (H) 18
   - (J) 3

7. $9^2 =$
   - (A) 90
   - (B) 81
   - (C) 18
   - (D) 3

8. $\sqrt{196} =$
   - (F) 14
   - (G) 15
   - (H) 16
   - (J) 17

9. $\sqrt{676} =$
   - (A) 23
   - (B) 24
   - (C) 25
   - (D) 26

10. $\sqrt{25} + \sqrt{9} =$
   - (F) $\sqrt{16}$
   - (G) $\sqrt{34}$
   - (H) $\sqrt{64}$
   - (J) none of the above

11. **100 =**
   - (A) 10^2
   - (B) 4×5^2
   - (C) $\sqrt{10,000}$
   - (D) all of the above

STOP

Name _____ Date _____

Mathematics

Commutative, Associative, and Distributive Properties

Number and Operations

DIRECTIONS: Choose the best answer.

The **commutative property** states that numbers can be added or multiplied in any order without changing the result. The **associative property** states that changing the grouping of numbers that are being added or multiplied does not change the result. The **distributive property** states that if a term is multiplied by terms in parentheses, the multiplication needs to be "distributed" over all the terms inside.

DIRECTIONS: For questions 1–5, tell which property is used to find each answer.

1. $-12x(4y \times 8z) = -12x(8z \times 4y)$ _____

2. $-12x(4y \times 8z) = (-12x \times 4y)8z$ _____

3. $-15x(-3x + 3) = 45x^2 - 45x$ _____

4. $-12x + (4y + 8z) = -12x + (8z + 4y)$ _____

5. $-12x + (4y + 8z) = (-12x + 4y) + 8z$ _____

DIRECTIONS: For questions 6–11, find the answer using the property indicated.

6. Use the commutative property to write an equivalent expression to $4.5x + 3y$.

_____

7. Use the associative property to write an equivalent expression to $(a + 17b) + 12c$.

_____

8. Use the distributive property to simplify $11x(2x + 5)$.

_____

STOP

Mathematics

| 1.C |

Analyzing Algorithms
Number and Operations

DIRECTIONS: For questions 1–4, use the algorithms described below to choose the best answers.

> One algorithm for dividing fractions is: (1) Flip the second fraction to get its reciprocal. Then, multiply the numerators and the denominators to find the answer. *Example:* To find
>
> $\frac{10}{12} \div \frac{2}{4}$, flip $\frac{2}{4}$ to get $\frac{4}{2}$. Then, multiply 10×4 and 12×2, which gives
>
> you $\frac{40}{24}$.

1. $\frac{8}{10} \div \frac{1}{5}$

   (A) $\frac{4}{2}$ (C) $\frac{2}{8}$

   (B) $\frac{8}{2}$ (D) $\frac{8}{5}$

2. $\frac{1}{2} \div \frac{1}{3}$

   (F) $\frac{1}{5}$ (H) $\frac{5}{1}$

   (G) $\frac{2}{3}$ (J) $\frac{3}{2}$

> One algorithm for multiplying two numbers is: (1) break down one of the numbers into a simpler equation, (2) multiply the first number by the new second number, and (3) multiply the result by the new third number. *Example:* To multiply 25×36, break down one of the numbers into a simpler equation: $25 \times 4 \times 9$; multiply the first number by the new second number: $25 \times 4 = 100$; and multiply that result by the new third number: $100 \times 9 = 900$.

3. $12 \times 15 =$

   (A) 160

   (B) 200

   (C) 180

   (D) 220

4. 20×25 is the same as

   (F) $20 \times 5 \times 5$

   (G) $20 \times 20 \times 5$

   (H) $10 \times 10 \times 25$

   (J) $20 \times 4 \times 5$

5. In your own words, write an algorithm explaining how to convert a mixed number to a fraction. (For example, the mixed number $7\frac{1}{3}$ can be converted to a fraction $\frac{22}{3}$.) Provide an example.

_____

_____

_____

STOP

Name _____ Date _____

Mathematics

Linear and Nonlinear Functions

Algebra

Clue

A **linear function** is an equation whose graph is a straight line. The equations of linear functions can be written as $y = mx + b$; for example, $y = x + 4$, $y = -4$, and $3x - 4y = \frac{1}{2}$ are linear functions.

An equation whose graph is not a straight line is called a **nonlinear function.** There are many kinds of nonlinear functions. Examples are $y = ax^2 + bx + c$ and $y = ax^3 + bx^2 + cx + d$ (where $a \neq 0$).

DIRECTIONS: Tell if the following functions are linear or nonlinear.

1. $y = 5x - 3$ _____

2. $y = 3x^2 - 4$ _____

3. $y = 2x - 1$ _____

4. $y = 4x + 2$ _____

5. $y = -x^2$ _____

6. $y = 7x^2 + 3x + 21$ _____

DIRECTIONS: Choose the best answer.

7. **Which function corresponds to this table?**

x	0	1	2
y	1	4	7

   (A) $y = 3x + 1$

   (B) $y = x^3 + 1$

   (C) $y = 3x - 1$

   (D) $y = x^2 - 1$

8. **Which function corresponds to this table?**

x	0	1	2	3
y	0	2	10	30

   (F) $y = 6x + 12$

   (G) $y = x^2 + x$

   (H) $y = 6x - 2$

   (J) $y = x^3 + x$

9. **Which function corresponds to the following graph?**

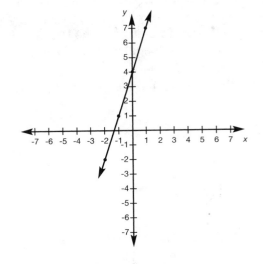

   (A) $y = -x^2 + 4$

   (B) $y = 3x + 4$

   (C) $y = -0.25x^2 + 4$

   (D) $y = 0.25x + 4$

STOP

Mathematics

2.B

Slope and Intercept
Algebra

Clue An **intercept** is a point on a graph where a line or curve crosses an axis. The x-intercept is where the line crosses the x axis; the y-intercept is where the line crosses the y axis. In the illustration below, the x-intercept is the point (2, 0) and the y-intercept is the point (0, 3).

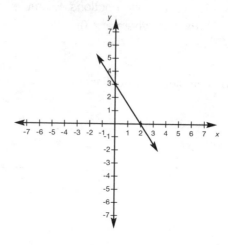

Follow these steps to graph linear functions using intercepts:

Step 1: Find the x- and y- intercepts. Find the x-intercept by plugging in 0 for y and solving for x; find the y-intercept by plugging in 0 for x and solving for y.

Step 2: Find one more point. To do this, use any value for x and find its equivalent y value.

Step 3: Plot the intercepts and points you found in steps 1 and 2, and then draw the line.

DIRECTIONS: Graph each linear function by finding the x- and y- intercepts.

1. $y = 5 - x$

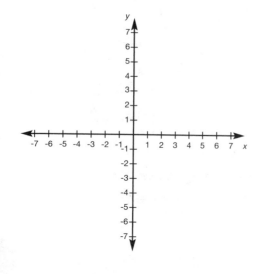

2. $3x - 2y = -6$

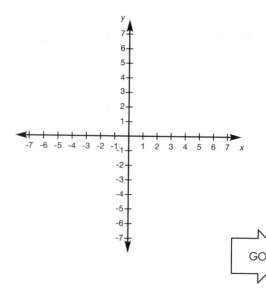

Name _____ Date _____

Clue The **slope** of a line measures the steepness of the line. **Rise** is how many units you move up or down from point to point; on a graph, rise indicates a change in the *y* values. **Run** is how far left or right you move from point to point; on a graph, run indicates a change in the *x* values. The formula below is used to find the slope of a line. The subscripts show that there are two different points. The letter *m* represents slope.

Slope Formula Given Two Points

Given two points (x_1, y_1) and (x_2, y_2)

$$m = \frac{\text{rise}}{\text{run}} = \frac{\text{change in y}}{\text{change in x}} = \frac{y_2 - y_1}{x_2 - x_1}$$

DIRECTIONS: Use the slope formula to find the slopes of the lines described below.

3. **Find the slope of the straight line that passes through (−5, 2) and (4, −7).**

_____

4. **Find the slope of the straight line that passes through (1, 1) and (5, 1).**

_____

5. **Find the slope of the line shown in the graph.**

_____

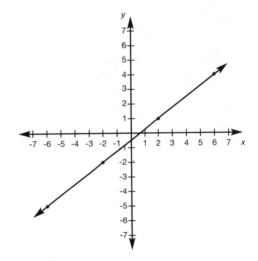

6. **Find the slope of the lines you drew in questions 1 and 2.**

_____

_____

STOP

Name _____ Date _____

[2.C]

Modeling and Solving Problems
Algebra

DIRECTIONS: Read the scenario below and then answer the questions that follow.

Clue — A line of best fit is a line drawn on a scatterplot of data that is closest to most points of the scatterplot. This line may pass through some of the points, none of the points, or all of the points. In the equation for a straight line $y = mx + b$, m is the slope of the line and b is the y-intercept.

Janine recorded the time it took for candles of different lengths to burn out. She recorded her results in the following table.

Candle Length (in inches)	2.0	2.4	3.5	3.0	3.0	2.7
Burning Time (in minutes)	18	19	28	24	25	22

1. On the grid below, create a scatterplot of Janine's data and then draw a line of best fit for the data.

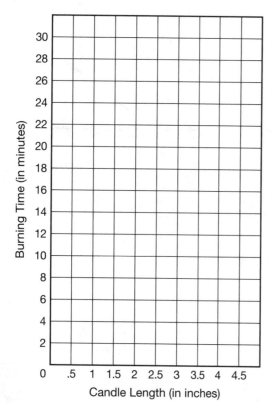

2. Write an equation for the line of best fit.

_____

3. Find the slope for the line you drew in question 1.

_____

4. Explain what the slope represents within the context of this problem.

_____

_____

_____

STOP

Mathematics

2.D

Creating a Table of Values and Plotting Points for Linear Equations

Algebra

DIRECTIONS: Choose the best answer.

1. For the linear equation $y = 3x + 2$, find the corresponding y values when x = −3, −2, −1, 0, 1, 2, and 3. Show the results as a table of values.

x							
y							

2. For the linear equation $y = 2x$, find the corresponding y values when x = −3, −2, −1, 0, 1, 2, and 3. Show the results as a table of values.

x							
y							

3. Plot the points on the Cartesian plane for the equation given in question 1.

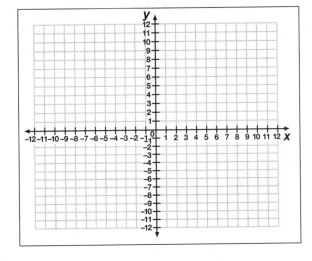

4. Plot the points on the Cartesian plane for the equation given in question 2.

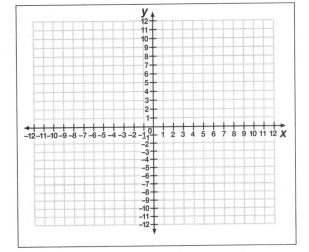

STOP

Mathematics

$\boxed{\textbf{1.0–2.0}}$

For pages 44–53

Mini-Test 1

Number and Operations; Algebra

DIRECTIONS: Uncle Albert's attic contains 5 boxes of old records, 7 boxes of old books, 3 radios, 4 boxes of holiday decorations, and 2 paintings. Use this information to answer questions 1 and 2.

1. **What is the ratio of radios to boxes of old records in Uncle Albert's attic?**

   - (A) 5:3
   - (B) 1:3
   - (C) 3:5
   - (D) 3:8

2. **Suppose the number of paintings increases by two. If everything else in the attic increases by the same proportion, how many boxes of holiday decorations will there be?**

   - (F) 2
   - (G) 4
   - (H) 6
   - (J) 8

DIRECTIONS: Choose the best answer.

3. **The square root of 12 is between which two whole numbers?**

   - (A) 3 and 4
   - (B) 4 and 5
   - (C) 5 and 6
   - (D) 6 and 7

4. **If you use the commutative property to write an equivalent expression to $\frac{4}{7} \times \frac{x}{8}$, you will get**

   - (F) $4x \times 15$
   - (G) $\frac{4}{8} \times \frac{7}{x}$
   - (H) $\frac{x}{8} \times \frac{4}{7}$
   - (J) $\frac{4}{7x} \times 8$

5. **Which of the following equations will not result in a straight line when graphed?**

   - (A) $y = 2x - 2$
   - (B) $y = 3x^2 - 7$
   - (C) $y = 12x - 12$
   - (D) $y = x + 2$

6. **$43.24 \times 10^5 =$**

   - (F) 43,240
   - (G) 432,400
   - (H) 4,324,000
   - (J) 43,240,000

7. **Graph the linear function $y = 7 - 2x$ by finding the x- and y- intercepts.**

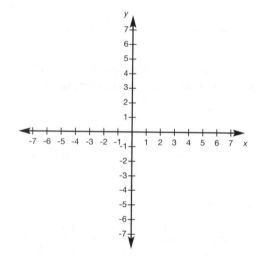

8. **Find the slope for the line you drew in question 7.**

_____

STOP

Mathematics

3.A

Making and Testing Conjectures

Geometry

DIRECTIONS: Answer the following questions. If necessary, test your idea before answering by drawing various shapes.

 The length of any side of a triangle is less than or equal to the sum of the lengths of the other two sides. This is called **triangle inequality**.

1. Can a triangle have the following measures: 4, 9, and 8? Explain.

_____

_____

_____

_____

2. Can a triangle have the following measures: 10, 18, and 7? Explain.

_____

_____

_____

_____

 Complementary angles add up to 90°. **Supplementary angles** add up to 180°.

3. In a parallelogram, are the adjacent angles complementary or supplementary? Write your answer, then draw a parallelogram and test your conjecture.

_____

_____

_____

_____

4. Which sides of a parallelogram ABCD are equal in length? Write your answer, then draw a parallelogram and test your conjecture.

_____

_____

_____

_____

STOP

Name _____ Date _____

Mathematics

Justifying Theories About Angles

Geometry

DIRECTIONS: Answer the following questions. If necessary, test your idea before answering by drawing various shapes.

 Clue   The angles are identified with the symbol ∠.

1. **Examine the figure below. Use what you know about angles to prove that ∠1 = ∠2. Do not measure the angles. Complete the table below to help you find your answers. Fill in the missing formulas under the Statement column and the missing justifications under the Reason column. Some of the entries have been completed for you.**

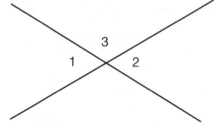

Statement	Reason
∠1 + ∠3 = 180° ∠2 + ∠3 = 180°	
If the above statements are true, then:	Substitution
If the above statements are true, then:	Algebra

2. **Construct a triangle out of paper. Then, cut off the corners and arrange them so that their angles meet at the vertex to form a straight line. What have you just proven? Explain your answer.**

_____

_____

_____

 STOP

Mathematics

3.B

Using Coordinate Geometry to Examine Geometric Shapes

Geometry

DIRECTIONS: Use the coordinate grids to find the answers.

1. Points *A, B, C,* and *D* have these coordinates: *A* (3, 4), *B* (−2, 4), *C* (−2, 2), and *D* (3, 2). Find the area of quadrilateral *ABCD*.

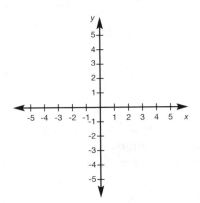

(A) 14   (C) 7

(B) 10   (D) 5

3. Points *A, B, C,* and *D* have these coordinates: *A* (3, 2), *B* (3, −2), *C* (−3, −2) and *D* (−3, 0). Find the area of quadrilateral *ABCD*.

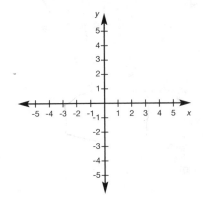

(A) 12   (C) 18

(B) 15   (D) 21

2. Points *A, B,* and *C* have these coordinates: *A* (0, 4), *B* (0, 0), and *C* (3, 0). Find the area of triangle *ABC*.

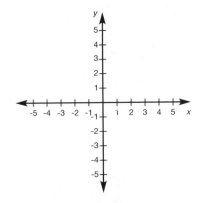

(F) 6   (H) 12

(G) 7   (J) 21

4. Points *G* and *H* have these coordinates: *G* (−3, 3) and *H* (−1, −1). What are the coordinates for the midpoint of $\overline{GH}$?

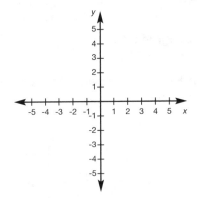

(F) (2, −1)   (H) (1, 2)

(G) (−2, 1)   (J) (−1, −2)

STOP

Mathematics
3.C
Similar and Congruent Figures
Geometry

DIRECTIONS: Triangles ABC and XYZ are congruent. Match each segment or angle below with its corresponding part.

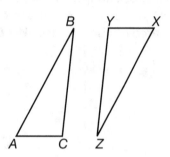

1. $\overline{AC}$ is congruent to _____ .

2. ∠XYZ is congruent to _____ .

3. $\overline{AB}$ is congruent to _____ .

4. ∠ABC is congruent to _____ .

5. ∠YZX is congruent to _____ .

6. $\overline{YZ}$ is congruent to _____ .

DIRECTIONS: Find the unknown measures *n* and *m* for these similar triangles.

7. *n* = _____

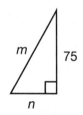

8. *m* = _____

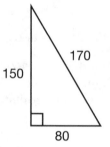

DIRECTIONS: Use the figure below to answer question 9.

9. **Points D, E, and F are vertices of an equilateral triangle; points J, K, and L are midpoints of its sides. Draw as many noncongruent triangles as you can using any three of these six points as vertices.**

STOP

Name _____   Date _____

Mathematics

Visualization, Spatial Reasoning, and Geometric Modeling

Geometry

DIRECTIONS: Use the figure below to answer questions 1 and 2.

1. **What is the surface area of the cube?**

   Ⓐ 24 cm²

   Ⓑ 54 cm²

   Ⓒ 67.5 cm²

   Ⓓ 81 cm²

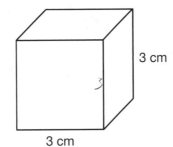

3 cm

2. **What is the volume of the cube?**

   Ⓕ 27 cm³

   Ⓖ 54 cm³

   Ⓗ 67.5 cm³

   Ⓙ 81 cm³

3 cm

DIRECTIONS: Use the figure below to answer question 3.

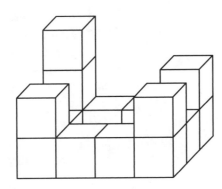

3. **Fifteen black cubes are put together to form the figure above. The complete surface of the figure, including the bottom, is painted white. The figure is then separated into individual cubes. How many of the individual cubes have exactly four white faces?**

   Ⓐ 4

   Ⓑ 6

   Ⓒ 7

   Ⓓ 10

GO

Name _____   Date _____

DIRECTIONS: Use the figure below to answer question 4.

4. Six cubes, each of which has a 10-cm edge, are joined together as shown above. Find the total surface area.

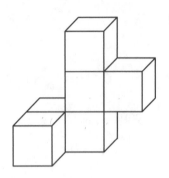

    (F)   2,400 cm²

    (G)   2,600 cm²

    (H)   3,000 cm²

    (J)   3,600 cm²

DIRECTIONS: Use the figure below to answer question 5.

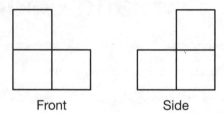

Front   Side

5. A figure is constructed from cubes, all of which have one-inch edges. Each cube shares at least one face with another cube. What is the minimum number of cubes needed to build a figure with the front and side views as shown above?

    (A)   4

    (B)   5

    (C)   6

    (D)   7

DIRECTIONS: Choose the best answer.

6. A circle and two distinct lines are drawn on a sheet of paper. What is the largest possible number of points of intersection of these figures?

    (F)   2

    (G)   3

    (H)   4

    (J)   5

STOP

Mathematics

| 4.A |

Understanding Relationships Among Units of Measurement

Measurement

DIRECTIONS: Choose the best answer.

1. One evening, you notice a flash of lightning. Ten seconds later, you hear thunder. Sound travels at 1088 feet per second. One mile is 5,280 feet. About how far were you from the lightning?

   (A) 1 mile

   (B) 2 miles

   (C) 3 miles

   (D) 4 miles

2. Molly had a gallon of milk. If she drank a pint, how many cups of milk were left in the container?

   (F) 4 cups

   (G) 3 cups

   (H) 6 cups

   (J) 14 cups

3. Ben is putting the finishing touches on a poster he is making. He wants to stick 300 metallic stars on the poster. If it takes him 2 seconds to attach one star to the poster, how many minutes will he need to finish the job?

   (A) 4

   (B) 6

   (C) 8

   (D) 10

DIRECTIONS: Use the following information to answer questions 4 and 5.

Maria has two 600 ml pitchers containing grape juice. One pitcher is $\frac{1}{3}$ full and the other pitcher is $\frac{2}{5}$ full. Maria adds water to fill each pitcher completely. Then she pours both pitchers into one large container.

4. What fraction of the mixture in the large container is grape juice?

   (F) $\frac{1}{8}$ (H) $\frac{11}{30}$

   (G) $\frac{3}{16}$ (J) $\frac{11}{15}$

5. How much liquid is in the large container?

   (A) 0.6 liters   (C) 6 liters

   (B) 1.2 liters   (D) 12 liters

DIRECTIONS: Choose the best answer.

6. A slug can travel 1 inch every 5 seconds. How far will the slug travel in a $\frac{1}{2}$ hour?

   (F) 10 inches   (H) 10 yards

   (G) 10 feet   (J) 10 miles

7. Yoko is driving at a speed of 162 feet per second. How fast is she traveling in miles per hour (mph)?

   (A) 162 mph   (C) 75 mph

   (B) 110 mph   (D) 45 mph

8. Which of these is the greatest volume?

   (F) 36 pints   (H) 4 gallons

   (G) 24 quarts   (J) 60 cups

STOP

4.A

Using Appropriate Units of Measurement

Measurement

DIRECTIONS: Choose the best answer.

1. **Which of the following units is a measurement of mass?**
   - (A) kilogram
   - (B) quart
   - (C) kilometer
   - (D) teaspoon

2. **Which of the following is a measurement of volume?**
   - (F) pound
   - (G) yard
   - (H) pint
   - (J) gram

3. **Angles are typically measured in _____ .**
   - (A) cubic feet
   - (B) degrees
   - (C) square feet
   - (D) arcs

4. **The distance around a figure is called _____ .**
   - (F) volume
   - (G) size
   - (H) mass
   - (J) perimeter

5. **The distance across a circle through its center is the _____ .**
   - (A) vertex
   - (B) circumference
   - (C) diameter
   - (D) volume

6. **A cubic meter is a measure of _____ .**
   - (F) volume
   - (G) weight
   - (H) length
   - (J) mass

7. **Which of these would be purchased by the ton?**
   - (A) gasoline
   - (B) gravel
   - (C) potatoes
   - (D) milk

8. **Which comes closest to the length of a loaf of garlic bread?**
   - (F) 1 meter
   - (G) 5 decimeters
   - (H) 180 millimeters
   - (J) 18 centimeters

DIRECTIONS: For each length or distance described below, write the unit of measurement—**mm, cm, m, or km**—that would be the most appropriate to use. (*Note:* One of the measurement units is used twice.)

_____ 9. **distance from Chicago to Atlanta**

_____ 10. **collar size**

_____ 11. **length from one side of a room to the other**

_____ 12. **length of your fingernail**

_____ 13. **skirt length**

STOP

Mathematics

4.B # Solving Measurement Problems
Measurement

DIRECTIONS: Choose the best answer.

1. Homer began peeling a pile of 44 potatoes at the rate of 3 potatoes per minute. Four minutes later, Bart joined him and peeled at the rate of 5 potatoes per minute. When they finished, how many potatoes had Bart peeled?

   Ⓐ 20
   Ⓑ 24
   Ⓒ 32
   Ⓓ 33

2. A cube has a volume of 8 cm³. Suppose the length of each side of the cube doubles. What is the volume of this new cube?

   Ⓕ 16 cm³
   Ⓖ 28 cm³
   Ⓗ 32 cm³
   Ⓙ 64 cm³

DIRECTIONS: Use the figure below to answer questions 3–5.

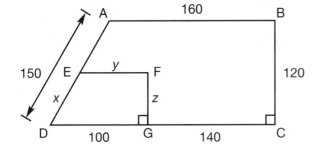

3. What is the value of x?

   Ⓐ $62\frac{1}{2}$
   Ⓑ $60\frac{5}{8}$
   Ⓒ 70
   Ⓓ $77\frac{1}{2}$

4. What is the value of y?

   Ⓕ $55\frac{1}{3}$
   Ⓖ 60
   Ⓗ $66\frac{2}{3}$
   Ⓙ $77\frac{1}{4}$

5. What is the value of z?

   Ⓐ 30
   Ⓑ $30\frac{7}{8}$
   Ⓒ $40\frac{1}{2}$
   Ⓓ 50

DIRECTIONS: Choose the best answer.

6. Dwayne rides 3 hours on a bicycle trip into the country and back. He rode out at the rate of 15 mph and returned at the rate of 10 mph. How far into the country did Dwayne ride?

   Ⓕ 15 miles
   Ⓖ 18 miles
   Ⓗ 30 miles
   Ⓙ 36 miles

7. A model replica of a building measures 5.2 inches tall, and the width of the base is 1.6 inches. If the actual building is 280 meters tall, about how wide is the actual base?

   Ⓐ 86.15 meters
   Ⓑ 125.45 meters
   Ⓒ 135.48 meters
   Ⓓ 173.91 meters

GO

8. **Find the perimeter of the figure below.**

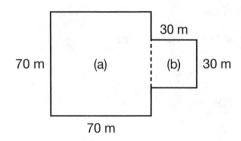

9. **Find the perimeter of the figure below.**

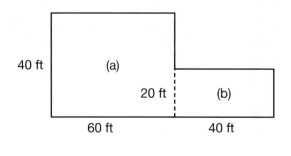

10. **Find the area of the figure below.**

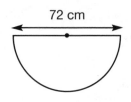

11. **Find the volume of the pyramid below.**

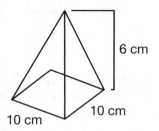

12. **Find the volume of the cylinder below.**

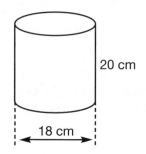

13. **Measure the angle below.**

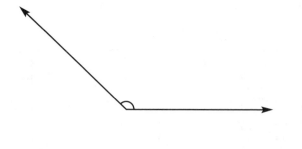

Name _____   Date _____

Mathematics

3.0–4.0

For pages 55–64

DIRECTIONS: Use the coordinate grid to answer question 1.

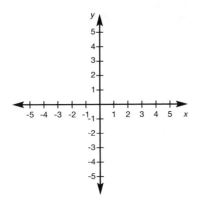

1. **Points *G* and *H* have these coordinates: *G* (−3, 3) and *H* (−1, −1). What are the coordinates for the midpoint of $\overline{GH}$?**

   (A) (−2, −1)

   (B) (−1, −1)

   (C) (−2, 1)

   (D) (1, −0.5)

DIRECTIONS: Choose the best answer.

2. **If two angles are supplementary and the measure of angle 1 is 34°, what is the measure of angle 2?**

   (F) 56°

   (G) 146°

   (H) 112°

   (J) 326°

3. **A broken pipe is leaking water at the rate of 2 pints per hour. It leaks for 2 days before it can be repaired. How many gallons of water were lost because of the leak?**

   (A) 96 gallons

   (B) 12 gallons

   (C) 4 gallons

   (D) 24 gallons

4. **Brianna counted the number of edges of a cube, Jose counted the number of corners, and Dylan counted the number of faces. They then added the three numbers. What was the resulting sum?**

   (F) 12

   (G) 16

   (H) 22

   (J) 26

5. **What is the volume of the figure below?**

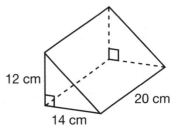

   (A) 1136 cm³

   (B) 1680 cm³

   (C) 3360 cm³

   (D) 23,520 cm³

DIRECTIONS: Use the figures below to answer question 6.

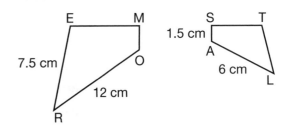

6. **Which line segment has a length of 3 cm?**

   (F) $\overline{MO}$

   (G) $\overline{ST}$

   (H) $\overline{TL}$

   (J) $\overline{ME}$

STOP

Name _____   Date _____

Using Histograms
Data Analysis and Probability

 Clue   A **histogram** is a bar graph that shows frequency data. An example of a histogram is shown below.

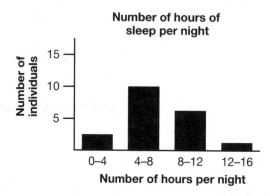

Number of hours of sleep per night

Number of individuals

15

10

5

0–4   4–8   8–12   12–16

Number of hours per night

The first step in making a histogram is to collect data and sort it into categories. Then, you need to label the data as the *independent variable* or the *dependent variable.* The characteristic you grouped the data by is the independent variable; the frequency of the data is the dependent variable.

Now you are ready to draw and label the histogram. The horizontal axis should be labeled with the independent variable; the vertical axis should be labeled with the dependent variable. Each mark on either axis should be in equal increments, such as 5, 10, 15, 20, etc. Then, you plot your data. Find the related frequency for each category and make horizontal marks to show the frequency.

DIRECTIONS: The data below represents the dollar sales (in millions) of 29 furniture stores in the state of Kentucky. You want to compare numbers of companies that make from $22.1 to $24.1 million; from $24.2 to $26.1 million; from $26.2 to $28.1 million; and so on. On a separate sheet of paper, create a histogram for this purpose.

32.1	38.9	42.1
27.4	24.1	28.5
27.8	36.6	27.1
61.8	34.6	42.9
27.8	24.9	36.7
27.0	27.3	25.2
25.9	34.1	28.4
27.1	56.5	25.5
34.2	45.8	40.9
28.0	28.5	

STOP

5.B

Mean, Median, Mode, Range, and Outliers

Data Analysis and Probability

DIRECTIONS: Use this data set for all the questions. Tanya's scores on a series of tests were: 83, 83, 64, 74, 74, 87, 82, 43, 76, 84, 94, 88.

Clue The **mean** of a set of data is the sum of the data divided by the number of pieces of data (average). The **mode** of a set of data is the number that occurs most often. The **median** of a set of data is the number in the middle when the numbers are put in order. The **range** of a set of data is the difference between the greatest value and lowest value of the set. The **outlier** for a set of data is any value that is markedly smaller or larger than other values.

1. **What would the median be if the two lowest scores were dropped?**

   Ⓐ 82

   Ⓑ 82.5

   Ⓒ 83

   Ⓓ 83.5

2. **What would the mean be if the two lowest scores were dropped?**

   Ⓕ 81

   Ⓖ 82.5

   Ⓗ 81.5

   Ⓙ 82

3. **What would the mode be if the two lowest scores were dropped?**

   Ⓐ 74, 83

   Ⓑ 74

   Ⓒ 83

   Ⓓ 82

4. **What would the median be if Tanya got 100 on her next test? Use all the scores.**

   Ⓕ 82

   Ⓖ 82.5

   Ⓗ 83.5

   Ⓙ 83

5. **What would the outlier be if Tanya got 100 on her next test? Use all the scores.**

   Ⓐ 43

   Ⓑ 64

   Ⓒ 94

   Ⓓ 100

6. **What would the range of the data be if Tanya got 100 on her next test? Use all the scores.**

   Ⓕ 30

   Ⓖ 51

   Ⓗ 36

   Ⓙ 57

STOP

Name _____ Date _____

Developing and Evaluating Inferences and Predictions

Data Analysis and Probability

DIRECTIONS: The box plots below show the distance John could throw a soft rubber ball and the distance he could throw a hard rubber ball. Use the box plots to answer question 1.

 Clue

The **box plots** show the extremes of the data for each type of ball. The line in each box is the median of the data.

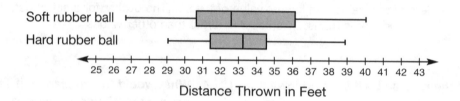

Soft rubber ball

Hard rubber ball

25 26 27 28 29 30 31 32 33 34 35 36 37 38 39 40 41 42 43

Distance Thrown in Feet

1. **From the above box plots, which type of ball can normally be thrown farther? Which type of ball is more variable in the distance it can be thrown?**

_____

_____

DIRECTIONS: The scatterplot below shows the distance of the Olympic gold medal winning high jump between the years 1900–1984. Use it to answer questions 2 and 3.

 Clue

A **line of best fit** is a straight line that best represents the data on a scatterplot. This line may pass through some of the points, none of the points, or all of the points.

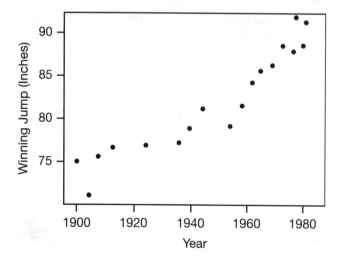

2. **Draw a line of best fit for the scatterplot.**

3. **What trend is illustrated by the data in the scatterplot? What prediction can you make for the winning high jump for the 1988 Olympics?**

_____

_____

_____

_____

STOP

5.D

Mutually Exclusive and Complementary Events
Data Analysis and Probability

 Clue

Two events are **mutually exclusive** if they cannot happen at the same time. Two events are **complementary** if one or the other must happen but they both can't happen.

DIRECTIONS: For each of the events listed below, tell if they are complementary or just mutually exclusive.

1. **you will get heads if you flip a coin or you will get tails**

   _____

2. **you roll a 1 on a die or you roll a 2**

   _____

3. **you roll an odd number on a die or you roll an even number**

   _____

4. **the next person you see will be a male or female**

   _____

5. **you get an A in English or you get a B in English**

   _____

DIRECTIONS: Choose the best answer.

6. **You select a page at random from this book. Which of the following are mutually exclusive pairs of events?**

   (A) The page is even-numbered/the page is numbered between 1 and 10.

   (B) The page is even-numbered/the page is numbered either 11 or 13.

   (C) Both A and B are mutually exclusive.

   (D) Neither A nor B are mutually exclusive.

7. **The probability of drawing a heart from a standard deck of cards is _____ .**

   (F) $\frac{4}{52}$ (H) $\frac{1}{2}$

   (G) $\frac{1}{4}$ (J) $\frac{3}{4}$

8. **What is the probability of the complement of the event in question 7?**

   (A) $\frac{48}{52}$ (C) $\frac{1}{2}$

   (B) $\frac{1}{4}$ (D) $\frac{3}{4}$

STOP

Solving Problems
Process

DIRECTIONS: Choose the best answer.

1. While Kenji is mowing his back yard, he wonders how much total area he is cutting. Which of the following will give him the answer?

   (A) area = 2 × 10 yd. + 2 × 20 yd.

   (B) area = 10 yd. × 20 yd.

   (C) area = 10 ft. × 20 ft.

   (D) area = 102 yd. × 202 yd.

2. Five people attend a dinner party. If every person shakes hands with all the other people at the party, how many handshakes will there be?

   (F) 8

   (G) 12

   (H) 6

   (J) 10

3. Suppose that a and b are positive numbers and that a > b. What is always true about the ratio (a × 2) ÷ (b × 2)?

   (A) The ratio is less than one.

   (B) The ratio is more than one.

   (C) The ratio is equal to one.

   (D) The ratio is a negative number.

4. Two truckers drove from Dayton to Toledo and back. The first trucker drove to Toledo at 50 mph and returned to Dayton at 60 mph. The second trucker drove to Toledo and back at 57 mph. If the round trip is 300 miles, which driver took longer to make the round trip?

   (F) first trucker

   (G) second trucker

   (H) they both took the same amount of time

   (J) not enough information

5. Marion owns a small construction company. Her job is to estimate the cost to build houses. One of the equations she uses is C = A × $89.00, where A is the area in square feet of the house and $89.00 is the average cost of construction per square foot. What do you think the C stands for?

   (A) the number of square feet in the house

   (B) the cost of finishing each room in the house

   (C) the real estate broker's commission

   (D) the building cost to the owner

6. In the circle below, the shaded portion represents the percentage of students who passed a fitness test. What percentage of students passed the test?

   (F) 80%

   (G) 75%

   (H) 40%

   (J) 20%

   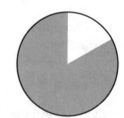

7. Players in the Big Gut Softball League buy socks and T-shirts. Socks cost $4 per pair and each T-shirt costs $5 more than a pair of socks. Each player needs one pair of socks and a shirt for home games and another pair of socks and a shirt for away games. If the total cost is $2,366, which of the following equations will tell how many players are in the league?

   (A) $2366 \div (4 + 5)^2 = n$

   (B) $2366 \div (4 + 9)^2 = n$

   (C) $2366 \div 26 = n$

   (D) $2366 \div 18 = n$

STOP

Name _____   Date _____

Mathematics

Using Mathematical Language
Process

DIRECTIONS: Choose the best answer.

1. The figure below is a _____ .

   (A) triangular prism

   (B) cube

   (C) rhombus

   (D) cylinder.

2. What label goes on the line on the Venn diagram below?

   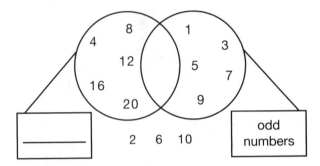

   (F) Prime numbers

   (G) Multiples of 4

   (H) Even numbers

   (J) Imaginary numbers

3. An angle formed by two adjacent sides inside a polygon is called a(n) _____ .

   (A) interior angle

   (B) adjacent angle

   (C) congruent angle

   (D) exterior angle

4. The radius of a circle is the _____ .

   (F) longest distance from one end of a circle to the other

   (G) center of the circle

   (H) distance around the circle

   (J) distance from the center of the circle to any point on the circle

5. All of the following triangles are classified by angle except _____ .

   (A) acute

   (B) scalene

   (C) right

   (D) obtuse

6. In the figure below, line segments $\overline{CG}$ and $\overline{AB}$ are _____ .

   (F) intersecting

   (G) parallel

   (H) skew

   (J) perpendicular

   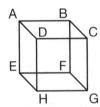

7. A flat surface that extends endlessly in all directions is a _____ .

   (A) quadrilateral

   (B) polygon

   (C) space

   (D) plane

8. In the term *2xy*, the number *2* is the _____ .

   (F) expression

   (G) coefficient

   (H) variable

   (J) constant

STOP

Applying Math to Other Areas

Process

DIRECTIONS: Choose the best answer.

1. Veronica had a submarine sandwich and a soft drink for $5.28. Logan ordered the same thing. Lily and Duncan split a pizza that cost $13.00 and each had a soft drink that cost $1.25. Which of the following would be the closest to a 20% tip on the total purchase?

   (A) $2.00

   (B) $2.50

   (C) $4.00

   (D) $5.00

2. Below is a diagram used by a framing company for determining the number of 1-inch by 1-inch tiles needed to frame a square trivet. The size of the square trivet below is 4 inches on each side. How many tiles are needed to frame it?

   (F) 16

   (G) 20

   (H) 18

   (J) 22

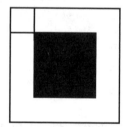

3. There are different time zones in the United States. When it is 9:00 P.M. in New York, it is 6:00 P.M. in California. If a plane leaves New York at 8:00 A.M. New York time and lands in California at 11:00 A.M. California time, how long was the flight?

   (A) 2 hours

   (B) 6 hours

   (C) 7 hours

   (D) 8 hours

4. The map below shows the distances between six cities in Pima County. Suppose you wanted to go from Mathtown to Circleville. What is the shortest distance you must travel?

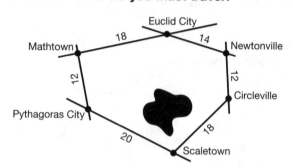

   (F) 30 miles

   (G) 50 miles

   (H) 44 miles

   (J) 64 miles

5. Ten square tables, each seating one person per side, are pushed together to form one long rectangular table. How many people can be seated?

   (A) 20

   (B) 22

   (C) 24

   (D) 28

6. Jackee entered the elevator on the floor where her mom is located. She went up 3 floors, down 3 floors, and up 10 floors. She got off the elevator to attend a meeting. After the meeting, she rode the elevator down 9 floors, up 4 floors, and finally down 6 floors to the first floor to eat in the restaurant. On what floor is Jackee's mom?

   (F) 4th floor

   (G) 2nd floor

   (H) 5th floor

   (J) 9th floor

STOP

Name _____ Date _____

Mathematics

6.E

Communicating
Mathematical Ideas

Process

DIRECTIONS: Choose the best answer.

1. For which of these equations would $a = 5$ when $b = 3$?

   (A) $ab = 12$

   (B) $a^2 = b^2 + 3$

   (C) $2a + b = 13$

   (D) $3a = b + 2$

2. The two soft drink bottles below are _____ .

   (F) neither congruent nor similar

   (G) congruent but not similar

   (H) similar but not congruent

   (J) similar and congruent

3. What number completes the following number sentence: $13 \times$ ___ $= 26 \times 20$

   (A) 18   (C) 26

   (B) 40   (D) 5

4. What is the missing weight in the balance below?

   (F) 2   (H) 6

   (G) 4   (J) 8

5. Jason is 6 feet tall and casts a shadow of 5 feet. If he stands next to a tree that casts a 10-foot shadow, how tall is the tree?

   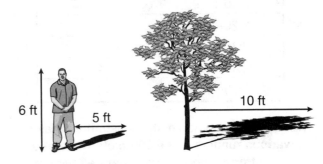

   (A) 10 feet

   (B) 12 feet

   (C) 14 feet

   (D) 8 feet

6. Two-thirds of the people in a room are seated in three-fourths of the chairs. The rest of the people are standing. If there are 6 empty chairs, how many people are in the room?

   (F) 18   (H) 27

   (G) 24   (J) 36

7. Amanda is making a pile of apples as shown below, with 1 apple in the first layer, 4 in the second, 9 in the third, 16 in the fourth, etc. If she makes 10 layers, how many apples will she use?

   (A) 250   (C) 400

   (B) 385   (D) 460

   STOP

Mathematics

5.0–6.0

For pages 66–73

Mini-Test 3

Data Analysis and Probability; Process

DIRECTIONS: Use the table below to answer question 1.

Time (min: sec)	Frequency
2:00–2:09	2
2:10–2:19	3
2:20–2:29	5
2:30–2:39	4
2:40–2:49	2
2:50–2:59	1

1. **The frequency table above lists the times of various runners in the 800-meter race at a recent track meet. On a separate sheet of paper, draw a histogram for the data.**

DIRECTIONS: Choose the best answer.

2. **Find the median of the following set of numbers: 4, 2, 3, 3, 3, 6.**
   - (A) 2
   - (B) 3
   - (C) 4
   - (D) 3.5

3. **Suppose the height of boys in your school was compared to the height of their fathers. In which prediction would you have greater confidence?**
   - (F) the prediction of the father's height from the son's height.
   - (G) the prediction of the son's height from the father's height
   - (H) equal confidence in both A or B
   - (J) not enough data to answer the question

4. **Which of the following are not complementary events?**
   - (A) a neighbor's new baby is a boy or a girl
   - (B) the number on a page is odd or even
   - (C) you pass a test or you fail a test
   - (D) you get 100% on a quiz or you get 90%

5. **A roll of tape contained 2 meters. If each box required 50 centimeters of tape, how many boxes could be secured with one roll of tape?**
   - (F) 2
   - (G) 4
   - (H) 6
   - (J) 8

6. **Reba has $750.00 in her bank account. The account earns 3% interest a year. Which equation will tell us how much money will be in the savings account at the end of the year?**
   - (A) $750 \times .03 = n$
   - (B) $750 + (750 \times .03) = n$
   - (C) $750 \div (.03 \times 750) = n$
   - (D) $750 \times .03 + .04 = n$

7. **The number of water lilies in a pond doubles each day. From the time one lily was placed in a pond until the time the pond was completely covered with lilies took 30 days. After how many days was the pond half covered?**
   - (F) 15 days
   - (G) 16 days
   - (H) 29 days
   - (J) not enough data to answer the question

STOP

How Am I Doing?

Mini-Test 1	8 answers correct	**Great Job!** Move on to the section test on page 76.
Page 54 **Number Correct**	5–7 answers correct	**You're almost there!** But you still need a little practice. Review practice pages 44–53 before moving on to the section test on page 76.
	0–4 answers correct	**Oops!** Time to review what you have learned and try again. Review the practice section on pages 44–53. Then, retake the test on page 54. Now, move on to the section test on page 76.
Mini-Test 2	6 answers correct	**Awesome!** Move on to the section test on page 76.
Page 65 **Number Correct**	4–5 answers correct	**You're almost there!** But you still need a little practice. Review practice pages 55–64 before moving on to the section test on page 76.
	0–3 answers correct	**Oops!** Time to review what you have learned and try again. Review the practice section on pages 55–64. Then, retake the test on page 65. Now, move on to the section test on page 76.
Mini-Test 3	7 answers correct	**Great Job!** Move on to the section test on page 76.
Page 74 **Number Correct**	5–6 answers correct	**You're almost there!** But you still need a little practice. Review practice pages 66–73 before moving on to the section test on page 76.
	0–4 answers correct	**Oops!** Time to review what you have learned and try again. Review the practice section on pages 66–73. Then, retake the test on page 74. Now, move on to the section test on page 76.

Final Mathematics Test
for pages 44–73

DIRECTIONS: Choose the best answer.

1. $6.12 \times 10^5 =$

   Ⓐ 60,210   Ⓒ 6,120,000

   Ⓑ 612   Ⓓ 612,000

2. Which of the following ratios are equal?

   Ⓕ 24:40 and 3:5

   Ⓖ 2:4 and 4:2

   Ⓗ 12:10 and 5:4

   Ⓙ 16:15 and 4:5

3. The square root of 71 is between which two whole numbers?

   Ⓐ 7 and 8

   Ⓑ 8 and 9

   Ⓒ 9 and 10

   Ⓓ 10 and 11

4. Use the distributive property to write $5(2x - y)$ without parentheses.

   Ⓕ $7x - 5y$

   Ⓖ $\dfrac{5}{2}x - 5y$

   Ⓗ $10x - 5y$

   Ⓙ $7x - y$

5. The only point on a graph that can be both an *x*- and *y*-intercept at the same time is _____ .

   Ⓐ (0, 0)   Ⓒ (1, 1)

   Ⓑ (1, 0)   Ⓓ (0, 1)

6. If slope $= \dfrac{1}{4}$ and y-intercept = 2, the equation for the line is _____ .

   Ⓕ $y = 2x + \dfrac{1}{4}$

   Ⓖ $y = \dfrac{1}{4}x - 2$

   Ⓗ $y = 2x - \dfrac{1}{4}$

   Ⓙ $y = \dfrac{1}{4}x + 2$

7. Which equation corresponds to the following table of values?

x	−2	0	2
y	−6	−3	0

   Ⓐ $y = 3x$

   Ⓑ $2x - 3y = 6$

   Ⓒ $3x - 2y = 6$

   Ⓓ $x = 3y$

DIRECTIONS: Use the graph below to answer questions 8 and 9.

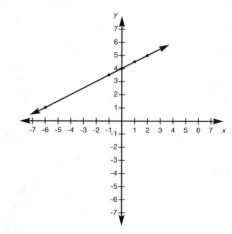

8. Which function corresponds to the line in the graph?

   Ⓕ $y = -x^2 + 4y$

   Ⓖ $y = -0.25x^2 + 2$

   Ⓗ $y = \dfrac{1}{2}x + 4$

   Ⓙ $y = 0.25x + 3$

9. What is the slope of the line in the graph?

   Ⓐ $\dfrac{1}{2}$

   Ⓑ $\dfrac{3}{4}$

   Ⓒ 1

   Ⓓ 2

GO

Name _____   Date _____

DIRECTIONS: Choose the best answer.

10. If two angles are supplementary and the measure of angle 1 is 26°, what is the measure of angle 2?

- (F) 19°
- (G) 64°
- (H) 154°
- (J) 334°

11. What is the missing measure in this triangle?

- (A) 30°
- (B) 50°
- (C) 60°
- (D) 90°

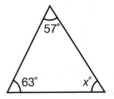

12. Find the volume of a square pyramid 6 feet high with a base 10 feet on a side.

- (F) 600 ft.^{3}
- (G) 300 ft.^{3}
- (H) 200 ft.^{3}
- (J) 100 ft.^{3}

13. The two figures below are similar. What is the perimeter of the larger figure?

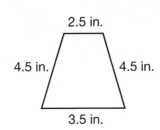
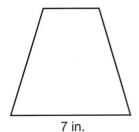

- (A) 30 in.
- (B) 28 in.
- (C) 22 in.
- (D) 15 in.

14. How many inches are in 13 feet?

- (F) 144
- (G) 156
- (H) 86
- (J) 13

15. Given the areas of the three squares in the figure, what is the area of the interior triangle?

- (A) 13
- (B) 30
- (C) 60
- (D) 300

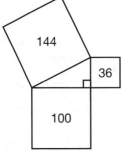

16. A bus was scheduled to leave the station at 3:15 P.M. Because of a rainstorm, the bus was delayed for 230 minutes. What time did the bus leave the station?

- (F) 6:30 P.M.
- (G) 6:50 P.M.
- (H) 7:05 P.M.
- (J) 7:15 P.M.

17. Which of the following best estimates the area of Tennessee?

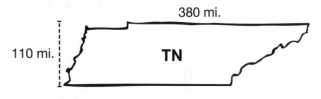

- (A) 41,800 mi.^{2}
- (B) 20,900 mi.^{2}
- (C) 30,000 mi.^{2}
- (D) 38,412 mi.^{2}

GO

18. What is the area of the region shaded below?

(F) 2.43 ft.²

(G) 4.54 ft.²

(H) 3.192 ft.²

(J) 9.42 ft.²

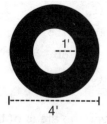

1'

4'

19. Mario drove his race car 217 miles per hour. How many feet per minute was the race car traveling?

(A) 10,400 ft. per min.

(B) 19,096 ft. per min.

(C) 16,084 ft. per min.

(D) 17,076 ft. per min.

20. The students in Ms. Fibonacci's math class collected data on how many hours of homework they do each week. Their results are shown in the table below. Which histogram correctly illustrates the data?

Frequency	Hours
6	0–4
6	4–8
10	8–12
2	12–16

(F)
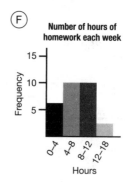

(G)
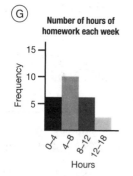

(H)
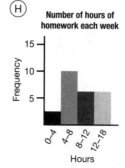

(J)
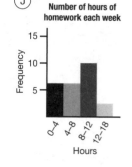

21. The distance from the center of a circle to any point on it is called the _____ .

(A) radius

(B) tangent

(C) chord

(D) diameter

22. What is the outlier in the following data set: 8, 17, 19, 20, 21, 22, 22, 22, 25, 26, 27, 28, 29

(F) 8

(G) 20

(H) 22

(J) 29

23. The gas tank in a car holds 22 gallons. It is now half full. If gas costs $2.39 a gallon, which equation will tell us how much will it cost to fill the tank?

(A) $22 \times \frac{1}{2} + 2.39 = n$

(B) $2.39 \times (22 \times \frac{1}{2}) = n$

(C) $2.39 \times (22 + \frac{1}{2}) = n$

(D) none of the above

DIRECTIONS: Use the coordinate grid to answer question 24.

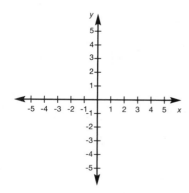

24. Points *P, Q,* and *R* have these coordinates: *P* (5, 2), *Q* (1, 0), and *R* (5, 0). What kind of triangle is *PQR*?

(F) equilateral

(G) right triangle

(H) scalene

(J) obtuse

STOP

Final Mathematics Test

Answer Sheet

1. Ⓐ Ⓑ Ⓒ Ⓓ
2. Ⓕ Ⓖ Ⓗ Ⓙ
3. Ⓐ Ⓑ Ⓒ Ⓓ
4. Ⓕ Ⓖ Ⓗ Ⓙ
5. Ⓐ Ⓑ Ⓒ Ⓓ
6. Ⓕ Ⓖ Ⓗ Ⓙ
7. Ⓐ Ⓑ Ⓒ Ⓓ
8. Ⓕ Ⓖ Ⓗ Ⓙ
9. Ⓐ Ⓑ Ⓒ Ⓓ
10. Ⓕ Ⓖ Ⓗ Ⓙ

11. Ⓐ Ⓑ Ⓒ Ⓓ
12. Ⓕ Ⓖ Ⓗ Ⓙ
13. Ⓐ Ⓑ Ⓒ Ⓓ
14. Ⓕ Ⓖ Ⓗ Ⓙ
15. Ⓐ Ⓑ Ⓒ Ⓓ
16. Ⓕ Ⓖ Ⓗ Ⓙ
17. Ⓐ Ⓑ Ⓒ Ⓓ
18. Ⓕ Ⓖ Ⓗ Ⓙ
19. Ⓐ Ⓑ Ⓒ Ⓓ
20. Ⓕ Ⓖ Ⓗ Ⓙ

21. Ⓐ Ⓑ Ⓒ Ⓓ
22. Ⓕ Ⓖ Ⓗ Ⓙ
23. Ⓐ Ⓑ Ⓒ Ⓓ
24. Ⓕ Ⓖ Ⓗ Ⓙ

Social Studies Standards

Standard 1—Culture *(See pages 81–82.)*
Social studies programs should include experiences that provide for the study of culture and cultural diversity.

Standard 2—Time, Continuity, and Change *(See pages 83–84.)*
Social studies programs should include experiences that provide for the study of the way human beings view themselves in and over time.

Standard 3—People, Places, and Environments *(See pages 85–87.)*
Social studies programs should include experiences that provide for the study of people, places, and environments.

Standard 4—Individual Development and Identity *(See pages 89–90.)*
Social studies programs should include experiences that provide for the study of individual development and identity.

Standard 5—Individuals, Groups, and Institutions *(See pages 91–92.)*
Social studies programs should include experiences that provide for the study of individuals, groups, and institutions.

Standard 6—Power, Authority, and Governance *(See pages 94–95.)*
Social studies programs should include experiences that provide for the study of how people create and change structures of power, authority, and governance.

Standard 7—Production, Distribution, and Consumption *(See pages 96–98.)*
Social studies programs should include experiences that provide for the study of how people organize for the production, distribution, and consumption of goods and services.

Standard 8—Science, Technology, and Society *(See page 99.)*
Social studies programs should include experiences that provide for the study of relationships among science, technology, and society.

Standard 9—Global Connections *(See pages 101–102.)*
Social studies programs should include experiences that provide for the study of global connections and interdependence.

Standard 10—Civic Ideals and Practices *(See pages 103–104.)*
Social studies programs should include experiences that provide for the study of the ideals, principles, and practices of citizenship in a democratic republic.

Name _____   Date _____

Social Studies

The Culture and Origins of the Australian Aborigine and New Zealand's Maori People

Culture

DIRECTIONS: Read the passages below, and then answer the questions that follow.

Australian Aborigine

Every tribe in Australia's Aboriginal population believes in Dreamtime—a time when the world was created and ancestral spirits roamed the earth.

During Dreamtime, the ancestors took the shapes of animals and plants and traveled across Australia. Their travels formed the rivers and rocks. They made people and left behind the spirits of all those who had yet to be born.

Through Dreamtime, Aborigines believe, all life is interconnected—past and present. These spiritual beliefs are the foundation for the political and social organization of the Aboriginal culture. Dreamtime was at the beginning of time and is ongoing, connecting all people, spirits, and the landscape itself, which is why the Aborigines believe their land is sacred.

New Zealand's Maori People

A great Maori sailor and fisherman from the legendary island of Hawaiki set out for a long ocean voyage. While out on the sea, instead of fish, he caught a giant island. It was too large to bring home, so the fisherman left it floating in the ocean. Generations later, another adventurous sailor set out to find the island. He had found a new home for many of his people—a land of mist and clouds.

Then, one tribal legend says, a fleet of seven canoes set out from Hawaiki about 1,500 years ago. Each tribe of Maori traces its ancestors back to one of the original canoes that brought their people to New Zealand.

Tribal stories tell that at death, the Maori spirits live on and journey back to Hawaiki, the spiritual homeland of the Maori people.

1. How do Aborigines explain how Australia came to be inhabited?

_____

_____

_____

2. How do the Maori explain how New Zealand came to be inhabited?

_____

_____

_____

3. Explain why the Australian Aborigines believe their land is sacred.

_____

_____

_____

4. What do you think the phrase "life is a journey from Hawaiki to Hawaiki" means to the Maori people?

_____

_____

_____

STOP

Social Studies

1.0

Transmission of Cultural Values Through Textbooks

Culture

DIRECTIONS: Read the passage and excerpts from *The New England Primer* below. Then, answer the questions that follow.

> *The New England Primer* was a small textbook first published in Boston around 1683. Most of the children of colonial America learned to read from this book. The *Primer* included rhymes, vocabulary words, short poems, and reading selections. Two typical excerpts are shown below.
>
> Good Children must,
> Fear God all day,   Love Christ alway,
> Parents obey,   In secret pray,
> No false thing say,   Mind little play,
> By no sin stray,   Make no delay,
>   In doing good.
>
> ***************************
>
> Awake, arise, behold thou hast
> Thy life, a leaf, thy breath, a blast;
> At night lie down prepar'd to have
> Thy sleep, thy death, thy bed, thy grave.

1. Identify at least two cultural values that are reflected in the excerpts.

   _____

   _____

   _____

2. Do you think the values communicated in the *Primer* were representative of colonial America in general? Why or why not?

   _____

   _____

   _____

3. What cultural values are reflected in the textbooks you are currently using? Give examples.

   _____

   _____

   _____

STOP

Name _____ Date _____

Social Studies

2.0

Changing Evaluations of Historical Events

Time, Continuity, and Change

DIRECTIONS: The following passage about slavery in America is from a history textbook used in American schools in the early 20th century. Read the passage and then answer the questions that follow.

> The negroes were generally quiet and good-natured. They went to work cheerfully, soon learned the English language and adopted the dress and customs of their masters. Certainly they fared better in America than they did in Africa, except that they were slaves, and for that they did not seem to care. . . .
>
> The southern planters brought the negroes from the slave traders, gave them comfortable homes in the slave quarters, and put them to work in the tobacco fields and the rice swamps. In this way a great slave system grew up in the South under circumstances which seemed fortunate and right at the time, and to which no one raised any objection. The negroes were generally well treated, were happy in their new homes, became devoted to their masters, and were satisfied with the condition that fate had awarded them.
>
> (Source: *First Lessons in American History,* by Lawton B. Evans. Published by Benj. H. Sanborn & Co., Boston, 1914, pp. 120–121.)

1. **How does the passage compare with what you have learned about slavery in America in your history classes?**

_____

_____

_____

2. **Do you think the passage is a credible and reliable description of the attitudes of slaves in America? Why or why not?**

_____

_____

_____

3. **Remember that this passage came from a textbook. How do you think it might have shaped students' perceptions of slavery in the early 20th century?**

_____

_____

STOP

Social Studies

| 2.0 |

Interpreting Time Lines
Time, Continuity, and Change

DIRECTIONS: Study the time line below, which shows important events in the development of transportation in the United States. Then, answer the questions that follow.

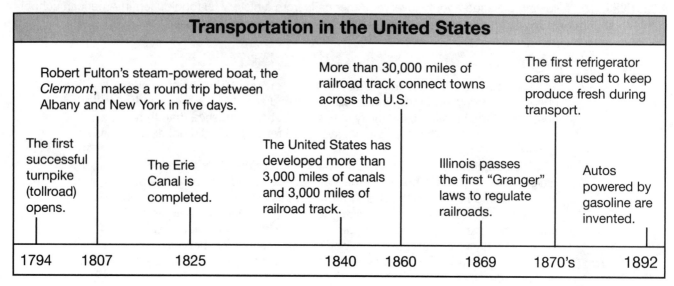

Transportation in the United States

Robert Fulton's steam-powered boat, the *Clermont*, makes a round trip between Albany and New York in five days.

More than 30,000 miles of railroad track connect towns across the U.S.

The first refrigerator cars are used to keep produce fresh during transport.

The first successful turnpike (tollroad) opens.

The Erie Canal is completed.

The United States has developed more than 3,000 miles of canals and 3,000 miles of railroad track.

Illinois passes the first "Granger" laws to regulate railroads.

Autos powered by gasoline are invented.

1794   1807   1825   1840   1860   1869   1870's   1892

1. **Which happened earliest?**

    (A) Autos chugged across the country.

    (B) Illinois passed a law to regulate railroads.

    (C) Robert Fulton's boat sailed.

    (D) The U.S. laid more than 3,000 miles of railroad track.

2. **How many years after 3,000 miles of track had been laid did Illinois pass a law to regulate railroads?**

    (F) 9 years

    (G) 29 years

    (H) 49 years

    (J) 59 years

3. **During which year is a transportation milestone not related to land travel listed?**

    (A) 1794

    (B) 1825

    (C) 1860

    (D) 1869

4. **Which event on the time line do you think had the greatest impact on increasing national markets for fruits and vegetables? Explain your answer.**

    _____

    _____

    _____

    _____

    _____

STOP

Name _____ Date _____

Social Studies

| 3.0 |

Identifying Landforms and Waterways
People, Places, and Environments

DIRECTIONS: Write a definition for each of the landforms and waterways listed below. Then, match each numbered feature on the map to the correct name for that feature. The first one has been completed for you.

___11___ **mountains:** ___very high natural___

___elevations___

_____ **lake:** _____

_____ **isthmus:** _____

_____ **bay:** _____

_____ **peninsula:** _____

_____ **strait:** _____

_____ **cape:** _____

_____ **island:** _____

_____ **gulf:** _____

_____ **sea:** _____

_____ **archipelago:** _____

_____ **ocean:** _____

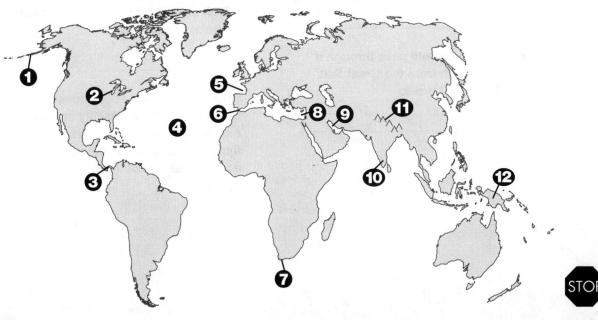

STOP

Social Studies

3.0

Mental Mapping
People, Places, and Environments

DIRECTIONS: Find a map of the United States and study it for a few moments. Then, put it aside and answer the following questions without consulting the map.

A **mental map** is a map of an area you have in your mind. It represents the perceptions and knowledge you have of an area. When you study a region of the world, try to picture its shape in your mind. Think about its most important cities and features and try to remember where they are located in relation to one another.

1. **Name three states that are west of the Mississippi River. Name three states that are east of this river.**

    _____

    _____

    _____

2. **Is Iowa north or south of Missouri?**

    _____

3. **What three states are bordered on the west by the Pacific Ocean?**

    _____

    _____

    _____

4. **Name the states you would pass through if you traveled due north from the Great Salt Lake to the Canadian border.**

    _____

5. **Name two states that share a border with one of the Great Lakes.**

    _____

    _____

6. **Five states share a border with the Gulf of Mexico. Name three of them.**

    _____

    _____

    _____

7. **Is North Dakota east or west of Minnesota?**

    _____

8. **Which is farthest west: North Carolina, West Virginia, or Kentucky?**

    _____

9. **On a separate sheet of paper, draw a mental map of your state. Identify important cities and features (such as rivers, lakes, etc.). Include a map key. Make your map as accurate as possible.**

STOP

Name _____   Date _____

Social Studies

Language Distribution
People, Places, and Environments

DIRECTIONS: The map below shows the primary language families spoken in Europe. Study the map and use it to answer the questions that follow.

Clue

A **language family** is a collection of languages that share common sources and are related in some important ways. Language families change and evolve over time and eventually become individual languages. For example, the English and Dutch languages are both part of the Germanic language family.

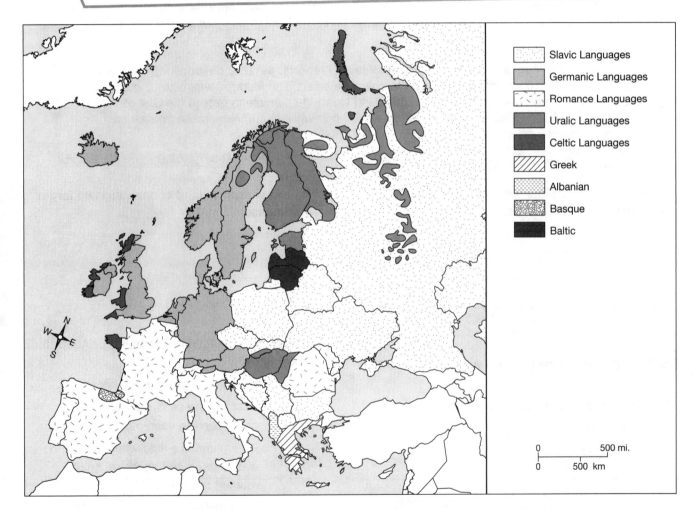

Legend:
- Slavic Languages
- Germanic Languages
- Romance Languages
- Uralic Languages
- Celtic Languages
- Greek
- Albanian
- Basque
- Baltic

0 ____ 500 mi.
0 ____ 500 km

1. **What is the predominant language family in eastern Europe?**

   _____

2. **Most of the people in France speak a language that is part of what language family?**

   _____

3. **What are the two main language families in the British Isles?**

   _____

4. **The map shows two different language families spoken in Spain. Identify them.**

   _____

Social Studies

| 1.0–3.0 |

For pages 81–87

Mini-Test 1

**Culture; Time, Continuity, and Change;
People, Places, and Environments**

DIRECTIONS: Read the following accounts of the Gulf of Tonkin incident, which took place during the Vietnam War. Then, answer question 1.

Account A
The U.S. government reported that on the evening of August 2, 1964, three North Vietnamese PT boats attacked without provocation the U.S. destroyer *Maddox*. The *Maddox* was routinely patrolling international waters about 30 miles off the coast of North Vietnam, in the Gulf of Tonkin. The *Maddox* and support aircraft returned fire; the North Vietnamese vessels retreated.

Account B
On the night of August 2, 1964, according to several reports, the U.S. destroyer *Maddox* was between 4 and 10 miles from the North Vietnamese coast. The *Maddox* was providing cover for South Vietnamese gunboats that were attacking North Vietnamese targets in the Gulf of Tonkin. The *Maddox's* log indicated that the *Maddox* fired first while North Vietnamese boats were approximately 6 miles away.

1. **In what ways do the two accounts differ? List at least two differences.**

   _____

   _____

   _____

   _____

DIRECTIONS: Choose the best answer.

2. **Which state does not border Mexico?**
   - (A) Arizona
   - (B) California
   - (C) Texas
   - (D) Louisiana

3. **This state lies between Minnesota and Iowa on the west and Lake Michigan on the east.**
   - (F) Illinois
   - (G) Wisconsin
   - (H) Indiana
   - (J) Ohio

4. **A narrow strip of land connecting two larger landmasses is a(n) _____ .**
   - (A) isthmus
   - (B) peninsula
   - (C) strait
   - (D) archipelago

5. **Which of the following is a belief of Australia's Aborigines?**
   - (F) Hawaiki is their spiritual homeland.
   - (G) Past and present lives have no connection to each other.
   - (H) Dreamtime is a time when the world was created and ancestral spirits roamed the earth.
   - (J) all of the above

6. **The Slavic languages are the predominant language family in _____ .**
   - (A) western Europe
   - (B) eastern Europe
   - (C) northern Europe
   - (D) none of the above

STOP

Name _____ Date _____

4.0

Theories of Identity Development
Individual Development and Identity

DIRECTIONS: Read the passage below, and then answer the questions that follow.

> Many psychologists have studied how people develop a sense of identity. Two researchers who studied identity development are Erik Erikson and James Marcia. Erikson believed that social and cultural factors have a strong influence on identity development, especially in adolescents. He thought that peers, or friends of the same age, were one of the most important influences.
>
> James Marcia identified four paths to identity development in adolescents. People on the first path are committed to the values of their parents or other adults without exploring their own identity. Those on the second path aren't sure about their values but are exploring their identity. People on the third path don't have a strong sense of self or values and aren't actively trying to find their identity. Those on the fourth path have explored their identity and have determined what their own values are.

1. **Do you agree with Erikson that peers are one of the most important influences on identity? Why or why not?**

   _____

   _____

   _____

   _____

2. **Which of Marcia's paths to identity do you feel that you are on? Explain.**

   _____

   _____

   _____

   _____

3. **Who or what do you think has had the strongest influence on your values?**

   _____

   _____

   _____

   _____ STOP

Social Studies

| 4.0 |

Connections to Places
Individual Development and Identity

DIRECTIONS: Answer the questions.

1. **Think of your favorite place in the world. On the lines below, describe it and explain why it is so important to you.**

_____

_____

_____

_____

_____

2. **Where did your parents or other adult family members grow up? Have you visited any of those places? Do you feel any special connection to those places? Why or why not?**

_____

_____

_____

_____

_____

3. **What is your family's ancestry? (*Ancestry* refers to the nationalities or ethnic groups from which you are descended—your heritage or "roots.") Do you especially identify with any of the homelands of your ancestors? Why or why not?**

_____

_____

_____

_____

4. **Do you and your family observe any special traditions associated with the homelands of your ancestors? If so, describe them. If not, why do you think these traditions are no longer observed?**

_____

_____

_____

_____

_____

STOP

Social Studies

| 5.0 |

Group Identity
and Social Class

Individuals, Groups, and Institutions

DIRECTIONS: Answer the following questions as completely as possible.

1. With which ethnic group do you most closely identify? To which social class would you say you belong?

   _____

2. When you watch TV or read newspapers or magazines, are people of your ethnic group, gender, and social class widely represented?

   _____

3. When you study the history of America in school, do you learn about the contributions of people of your ethnic group? Your gender? Your social class?

   _____

   _____

4. If you ask to speak with the manager of an institution such as a bank, a retail store, or another place of business, how likely is it that you will meet someone of your ethnic background or gender?

   _____

   _____

5. How many of your teachers share your ethnic background?

   _____

6. Can you readily purchase greeting cards that feature people of your ethnic group or social class?

   _____

7. If you cut your finger, can you easily find bandages that match the color of your skin?

   _____

8. What conclusions can you draw about group identity and social class from your answers to questions 1–7?

   _____

   _____

   _____

   _____

STOP

Social Studies

5.0

Tensions Between Belief Systems and Governments

Individuals, Groups, and Institutions

DIRECTIONS: Read the passage below, and then answer the questions that follow.

Jehovah's Witnesses are members of an international religious organization numbering more than 6 million. Witnesses are urged to obey the law and pay taxes. However, their religious beliefs have sometimes caused them to come into conflict with government. For example, Witnesses are forbidden to salute the flag, say the Pledge of Allegiance, or sing patriotic songs. Witnesses refuse to serve in the military. They are also urged not to vote, participate in political parties, or to run for elected office. For these reasons, Witnesses have sometimes been accused by governments of being "bad citizens."

Jehovah's Witnesses also believe that blood transfusions are immoral. Many Witnesses have refused to allow their sick or injured children to receive blood transfusions. Courts have sometimes overridden the wishes of parents and ordered transfusions for young children over the objections of their parents.

Despite the controversies, many scholars have argued that Jehovah's Witnesses have had a great influence on the promotion of civil rights around the world. These scholars believe that Witnesses have helped defend religious freedom and have therefore broadened the rights of millions of people.

1. **Which of the following do Jehovah's Witnesses refuse to do because of their religious beliefs?**

   (A) obey speed limit laws

   (B) pay property taxes

   (C) actively campaign for a political candidate

   (D) all of the above

2. **Which of the following best expresses the beliefs of Jehovah's Witnesses regarding patriotic songs?**

   (F) Witnesses believe such songs should be banned.

   (G) Witnesses believe such songs should be sung only on national holidays.

   (H) Witnesses believe only patriotic songs about America are acceptable; singing songs about other nations should be illegal.

   (J) Witnesses do not object to others singing patriotic songs, but they do not want to be forced to do so themselves.

3. **Do you believe it is appropriate for a government to force Jehovah's Witnesses to give their children blood transfusions, even though this violates their religious beliefs? Why or why not?**

   _____

   _____

   _____

   _____

   _____

   _____

   _____

   _____

   _____

   _____

   _____

   STOP

Social Studies

| 4.0–5.0 |

For pages 89–92

Mini-Test 2

**Individual Development and Identity;
Individuals, Groups, and Institutions**

DIRECTIONS: Answer the questions.

1. **To which do you feel the greatest connection: your neighborhood, your hometown, the United States, the country where your ancestors came from, or Earth itself? Explain why you feel this way.**

_____

_____

_____

_____

_____

_____

_____

_____

_____

_____

2. **Describe a situation in which your personal beliefs were in conflict with the law or with the expectations of a group or institution to which you belong. Explain what happened and tell how the conflict was resolved.**

_____

_____

_____

_____

_____

_____

_____

_____

_____

_____

STOP

Name _____ Date _____

Social Studies

6.0 # Changing the Constitution
Power, Authority, and Governance

DIRECTIONS: Study the chart below, and then answer the questions that follow.

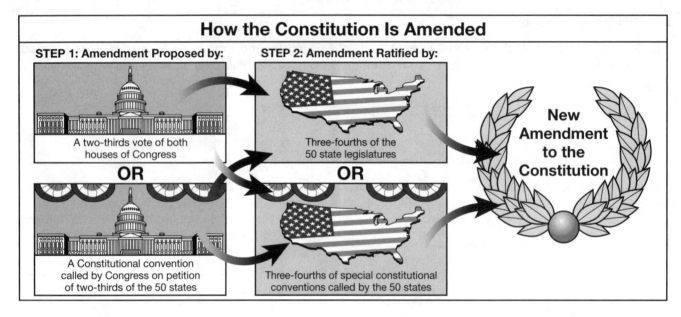

How the Constitution Is Amended

STEP 1: Amendment Proposed by:

A two-thirds vote of both houses of Congress

OR

A Constitutional convention called by Congress on petition of two-thirds of the 50 states

STEP 2: Amendment Ratified by:

Three-fourths of the 50 state legislatures

OR

Three-fourths of special constitutional conventions called by the 50 states

New Amendment to the Constitution

1. **Amendments to the U.S. Constitution must be ratified, or approved, by _____ .**

   (A) a two-thirds vote of both houses of Congress

   (B) three-fourths of the state legislatures

   (C) three-fourths of the state constitutional conventions

   (D) either B or C

2. **In order for a Constitutional convention to be called, how many states must request it?**

   (F) 25

   (G) 34

   (H) 38

   (J) 50

3. **The Twenty-Sixth Amendment gave the right to vote to _____ .**

   (A) African Americans

   (B) women

   (C) citizens of Washington, D.C.

   (D) citizens eighteen years of age or older

4. **Women received the right to vote in national elections as the result of the _____ .**

   (F) Fifteenth Amendment

   (G) Nineteenth Amendment

   (H) Equal Rights Amendment

   (J) Voting Rights Act of 1965

5. **Which of the following is true?**

   (A) The amendment process is quick and easy.

   (B) Most of the amendments that have been proposed have become part of the Constitution.

   (C) The amendment process has allowed the Constitution to be adapted to meet changing needs.

   (D) Amendments cannot be repealed.

Social Studies

| 6.0 |

The Electoral College
Power, Authority, and Governance

DIRECTIONS: Read the passage below, and then answer the questions that follow.

The electoral college was created by the Constitution because the Founding Fathers did not want the president to be elected by Congress or the people. It is a group of delegates chosen by the voters to elect the president and vice president. Each state has as many votes in the electoral college as it has senators and representatives in Congress. As a result, there are 538 electors, or delegates.

On Election Day, the first Tuesday after the first Monday in November, voters mark a ballot for president and vice president. They do not actually vote for the candidates, but they select electors to represent their state in the electoral college. The electors meet in December on a date set by laws to cast their votes. The results are sent to the president of the Senate who opens them. The public knows the results right after the November election because the news media figures them out. However, these results are not official until Congress has counted the electoral votes. After two representatives from each body of Congress have counted the votes, the results are officially announced in January. A candidate must receive 270 or a majority of the electoral votes to win. A candidate may win the popular vote but still lose the election.

1. **Who elects the president and vice president?**

   Ⓐ Congress

   Ⓑ the president of the Senate

   Ⓒ delegates chosen by the voters

   Ⓓ the voters themselves

2. **When are election results officially announced?**

   Ⓕ on Election Day

   Ⓖ later in November

   Ⓗ in December

   Ⓙ in January

3. **Why do some states have more votes in the electoral college than others?**

   Ⓐ They have more senators.

   Ⓑ They have more representatives in Congress.

   Ⓒ They have more land.

   Ⓓ They are the oldest states.

4. **What must a candidate receive in order to win?**

   Ⓕ 270 electoral votes

   Ⓖ 538 electoral votes

   Ⓗ a majority of the popular vote

   Ⓙ both F and H

5. **Explain why it is possible for a candidate to win the popular vote and still lose the election.**

   _____

   _____

   _____

   _____

   _____

   _____

   _____

STOP

Minimum and Maximum Wages

Production, Distribution, and Consumption

DIRECTIONS: Read the passage below, and then answer the questions that follow.

A **minimum wage** is the lowest legal wage a worker can be paid. A **maximum wage** is a limit on how much income an individual can earn. Both the minimum wage and the maximum wage are ways to redistribute wealth within a society.

Supporters of minimum wage laws argue that a minimum wage reduces low-paid work and distributes wealth more equitably within a society. They say that minimum wage laws put more money in workers' pockets, which increases their purchasing power and strengthens the economy. Supporters of a maximum wage say that it is unfair for top executives to make hundreds of times the annual pay of regular employees. Even executives at failing companies, they point out, often give themselves huge pay increases even as they lay off employees. This demoralizes lower-level workers and decreases their productivity on the job.

Opponents of the minimum wage argue that it actually destroys jobs and creates unemployment. They say that low-skilled workers need the opportunity to gain skills. If companies could pay lower wages, they would hire more employees. As a result, people would gain more work experience, which would allow them to progress up the economic ladder. Opponents of minimum wages also argue that employers are less likely to spend money on job training and other similar programs if they are forced to spend the money on wages instead. People who oppose maximum wage laws suggest that these laws reduce the incentive to work. People work hard because they expect to be rewarded for their hard work. Without this incentive, they argue, people would not work in difficult jobs or jobs that require high skills.

1. **Why do some people favor minimum wage laws? Do you agree with their arguments? Explain.**

_____

_____

_____

_____

2. **The United States currently has a minimum wage law, but not a maximum wage law. Do you think the United States should pass a maximum wage law? Why or why not? How do you think it would affect productivity in the United States?**

_____

_____

_____

_____

Name _____ Date _____

Social Studies

Labor Force and Gross Domestic Product
Production, Distribution, and Consumption

DIRECTIONS: The graphs below show the percentage of workers in each part of the Chinese economy and the percentage of the country's Gross Domestic Product (GDP) they produce. (GDP is the total value of goods and services produced by a nation.) Study the graphs and use them to answer the questions that follow.

China's Gross Domestic Product—By Sector

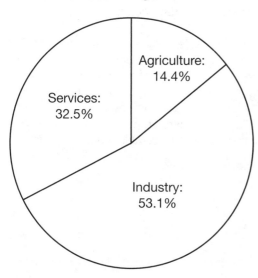

Agriculture: 14.4%

Services: 32.5%

Industry: 53.1%

China's Labor Force—By Occupation

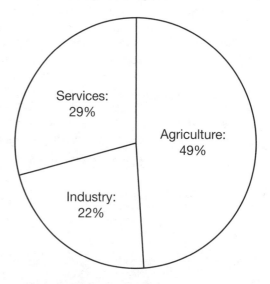

Services: 29%

Agriculture: 49%

Industry: 22%

1. How do the largest percentage of Chinese workers make a living?

_____

2. What makes up the largest percentage of China's GDP, and about what percentage of workers have jobs in that sector?

_____

3. What is the smallest segment of the Chinese GDP?

_____

4. True or false: The total number of Chinese working in industry and services is much greater than the total number of Chinese working in agriculture.

_____

5. Write a paragraph describing the relationship between the percentage of workers in each part of China's economy and the total goods and services they produce.

_____

_____

_____

_____

_____

_____

_____

_____

_____

_____

STOP

Name _____ Date _____

Social Studies

 7.0

The Consumer Price Index

Production, Distribution, and Consumption

DIRECTIONS: Read the passage below, and then answer the questions that follow.

> The Consumer Price Index (CPI) measures the average change over time in the prices consumers pay for a "market basket" of commonly used goods and services such as food, housing, clothing, medical care, recreation, school tuition—nearly everything people spend money on.
>
> The CPI is based on the spending of almost all residents of urban or metropolitan areas, including self-employed people, unemployed and retired persons, urban wage earners, and clerical workers. Not included in the CPI are the spending patterns of people who live in rural areas, farm families, and people serving in the armed forces.
>
> The CPI affects nearly all Americans because of the many ways it is used. For example, the CPI is the most widely used measure of inflation (the rate of increase in the general price level of all goods and services). Many analysts believe it indicates the effectiveness of government economic policy. In addition, the CPI is often used to adjust payments people receive from the government, such as Social Security payments. It is also used to adjust income eligibility levels for government assistance and to automatically provide cost-of-living wage adjustments to millions of American workers. Changes in the CPI also affect the cost of school lunches and are used to adjust the Federal income tax structure.

1. **What does the CPI measure?**

   _____

   _____

   _____

2. **List at least two ways that the CPI might affect a person's life.**

   _____

   _____

   _____

3. **What is the relationship between the CPI and inflation?**

   _____

   _____

   _____

4. **How might the reported CPI be different from your own personal experience with prices?**

   _____

   _____

   _____

STOP

Name _____ Date _____

Social Studies

8.0

Concerns About Scientific Advances

Science, Technology, and Society

DIRECTIONS: Read the passage below, and then answer the questions that follow.

> Many people have strong negative feelings about recent advances in biotechnology and genetic engineering. Two particular areas of concern are genetically modified (GM) foods and genetic cloning. GM foods are derived—in whole or in part—from organisms whose genetic material has been modified. Genetic cloning involves creating an identical genetic copy of an original. This can range from a single cell to an entire organism.
>
> Doubts about the safety of GM foods raise fears that scientists may have hurt the food supply. GM food products seem somehow "unnatural" to many consumers. Many people are also uneasy about the notion of genetic cloning. They are afraid that it may eventually lead to human cloning. Even if it does not lead to full-fledged human cloning, it might lead to gene enhancement, which could allow people, especially the wealthy, to pass on specific genetic traits to their offspring.

1. **Do you believe genetic cloning should be illegal? Is it acceptable for scientists to clone animals, but not humans? Explain your answer.**

   _____

   _____

   _____

   _____

2. **If science allows prospective parents to "select" certain traits they want their children to have—such as eye color or musical ability—do you think that should be permitted? Why or why not?**

   _____

   _____

   _____

   _____

3. **Could advances in biotechnology and genetic engineering cause some people to develop negative feelings toward scientific inquiry? Explain your answer.**

   _____

   _____

   _____

   _____

STOP

Social Studies

6.0–8.0

For pages 94–99

Mini-Test 3

Power, Authority, and Governance; Production, Distribution, and Consumption; Science, Technology, and Society

DIRECTIONS: Choose the best answer.

1. **Which of the following statements about amendments to the Constitution is true?**
   - (A) If an amendment is proposed by a two-thirds vote of Congress, it does not need to be approved by the states.
   - (B) Only state legislatures can approve amendments.
   - (C) Only Congress can propose amendments.
   - (D) Amendments can be repealed.

2. **The Nineteenth Amendment to the Constitution gave the right to vote to _____ .**
   - (F) former male slaves
   - (G) women
   - (H) citizens of Washington, D.C.
   - (J) citizens 18 years of age or older

3. **Under which of the following circumstances can a candidate be elected president in the United States?**
   - (A) If he receives a majority of the popular vote but not a majority of the electoral vote.
   - (B) If he receives a majority of the electoral vote but not a majority of the popular vote.
   - (C) If he receives a majority of both the electoral and popular votes.
   - (D) both B and C

4. **The lowest legal rate a worker can be paid is called a _____ wage.**
   - (F) equitable
   - (G) minimum
   - (H) fair
   - (J) maximum

5. **The total value of goods and services produced by a nation is called the _____ .**
   - (A) Gross Domestic Product
   - (B) National Debt
   - (C) Consumer Price Index
   - (D) Domestic Disposable Income

6. **The Consumer Price Index measures _____ .**
   - (F) the amount of money the average urban household has to spend after taxes
   - (G) the economic wealth of a nation
   - (H) the average amount of money a typical urban consumer spends in a year
   - (J) the average change over time in the prices of commonly used goods and services

7. **Which of the following individuals would be included in the measurement of the U.S. Consumer Price Index?**
   - (A) a farmer living in rural North Dakota
   - (B) a secretary living in Chicago, Illinois
   - (C) a captain in the U.S. Army
   - (D) all of the above

8. **Foods that are derived—in whole or part—from organisms whose genetic material has been altered are called _____ .**
   - (F) cloned foods
   - (G) frozen foods
   - (H) genetically modified foods
   - (J) Frankenstein foods

STOP

Name _____ Date _____

Social Studies

Free Trade
vs. Fair Trade

Global Connections

DIRECTIONS: Read the passages about free trade and fair trade below. Then, answer the questions on the next page.

A *tariff* is a tax that is charged on imported products. Tariffs raise the prices of imported goods, which makes them less competitive within the market of the importing country. A *subsidy* is a payment by a government to the producer of a good or service. Subsidies serve two purposes: they encourage the production of a good or service, and they reduce its cost to consumers.

FREE TRADE

Free trade refers to the elimination of tariffs, subsidies, and other barriers to the flow of products between countries. Supporters of free trade believe that it spreads knowledge, expands choices, and increases economic productivity. Because the market knows best, they argue, free trade works best when citizens have the freedom to participate in economic decision-making. This means that companies decide for themselves what to manufacture and how to market what they produce and consumers decide how to spend their own money.

Supporters of free trade believe that free trade leads to lower prices, higher employment, and greater productivity. They argue that success in free trade generates wealth, which raises the standard of living and allows people to become more self-sufficient. In such an atmosphere, claim free-trade supporters, authoritarianism becomes obsolete, and people begin to seek democratic reforms. As people get a taste of economic freedom, they begin to want political freedom as well.

FAIR TRADE

Some people are critical of free trade. They believe that unrestricted free trade benefits the wealthy at the expense of the poor. They argue that free trade has led to the rise of large multinational corporations. These corporations, they argue, exploit poor countries for their own economic gain. Multinational corporations may take the land of native people, which destroys their culture. Indeed, multinational corporations have become so powerful that they actually resemble small "nations," with power over the internal affairs of the underdeveloped nations in which they operate.

Critics of free trade encourage what they call *fair trade*. Fair trade promotes fair wages, environmental sustainability, financial and technical support, and respect for native cultures. Fair trade organizations (FTOs) try to benefit the producers they work with, not to maximize their own profits. Fair trade allows small producers to get their products to consumers with fewer "middlemen" in the process. This allows small producers to earn more revenue and still provide a good price for the customer. FTOs also work with producers to ensure safe working conditions and to give producers a voice in how their products are created and sold. Unlike multinational corporations, which take profits back to wealthy countries, FTOs encourage producers to reinvest profits in their own local communities.

GO

1. **What does the term *free trade* mean?**

   _____

   _____

   _____

   _____

2. **What arguments are used to support free trade?**

   _____

   _____

   _____

   _____

   _____

3. **In the 19th century, most American businesspeople favored tariffs. Now, most want tariffs to be eliminated. What do you think accounts for the difference?**

   _____

   _____

   _____

   _____

   _____

   _____

4. **How do you think fair-trade supporters feel about eliminating tariffs?**

   _____

   _____

   _____

   _____

   _____

   _____

5. **Do you think free trade promotes freedom in developing nations? Explain.**

   _____

   _____

   _____

   _____

   _____

   _____

6. **Which do you think offers the greater benefit to the United States, fair trade or free trade? Explain.**

   _____

   _____

   _____

   _____

   _____

STOP

Social Studies

| 10.0 |

Studying Media Reports
of Public Issues and Events

Civic Ideals and Practices

DIRECTIONS: Examine the Web sites of the following news organizations: *New York Times*, *New York Post*, CNN, FOX, Reuters, and a sixth of your choice (local newspaper, TV network, etc.) Visit the sites on the same day and roughly the same time. Use what you find on the sites to answer the following questions.

1. **What did each news organization feature as its lead/main story?**

   _____

   _____

   _____

   _____

2. **Find a story that is featured on every site. What is that story? Is the information the same on each site? If not, what are the differences? Do some sites highlight certain elements of the story while downplaying others?**

   _____

   _____

   _____

   _____

3. **What kinds of stories do each of these news organizations emphasize the most?**

   _____

   _____

   _____

   _____

4. **Which two sites do you think are the most different from each other? How do you think a viewer who relies on only one of these sites for information perceives today's issues and events differently from a viewer who uses the other?**

   _____

   _____

   _____

   _____

   _____

STOP

Name _____ Date _____

| 10.0 |

Understanding Political Parties' Views

Civic Ideals and Practices

DIRECTIONS: Go to the Web sites of the national Democratic, Libertarian, and Republican parties. Browse the sites and find out the position of each party on the issues listed in the table below. One good source would be each party's *platform* (official position statement) for the most recent presidential election. Do some additional research as needed. Then, summarize each party's position in the table. When the table is complete, highlight the positions with which you agree the most.

	Stem cell research	Restrictions on immigration	Elimination of estate tax	Health care reform
Democrat				
Libertarian				
Republican				

STOP

Social Studies

| 9.0–10.0 |

For pages 101–104

Mini-Test 4

Global Connections; Civic Ideals and Practices

DIRECTIONS: Choose the best answer.

1. **A political party's platform refers to** _____ .

   (A) the location of the party's national headquarters

   (B) the people who support the party

   (C) the party's official position statement on important issues

   (D) the place where candidates give speeches

2. **A tax charged on imported products is called a(n)** _____ .

   (F) tariff

   (G) embargo

   (H) subsidy

   (J) quota

3. **Which of the following is not an argument used by free-trade supporters to promote free trade?**

   (A) increased economic productivity

   (B) higher employment

   (C) environmental sustainability

   (D) higher standards of living

4. **One benefit of fair trade is that** _____ .

   (F) fair-trade products cost as much as 75% less than free-trade products

   (G) there are fewer middlemen between producers and consumers

   (H) it helps wealthy nations at the expense of developing nations

   (J) it allows multinational corporations to make tremendous profits

5. **Why do some people believe that free trade tends to make authoritarian governments obsolete?**

   (A) Success in free trade generates wealth, which allows people to purchase weapons to overthrow authoritarian governments.

   (B) Authoritarian leaders become so wealthy under free trade that they no longer need to dominate their people.

   (C) Democratic governments usually refuse to do business with authoritarian governments, so oppressive governments are forced to embrace democracy.

   (D) Success in free trade generates wealth, which raises the standard of living and allows people to become self-sufficient.

6. **Which of the following statements about American news organizations is true?**

   (F) American news organizations are all owned and operated by the federal government.

   (G) Newspapers are more accurate and reliable than television news reports.

   (H) The Republican Party owns all television news organizations; the Democratic Party owns all the newspapers.

   (J) Some American news organizations are owned and operated by foreigners.

7. **The news that the American media report every day** _____ .

   (A) is generally the same no matter the source

   (B) can vary greatly depending on the decisions news organizations make

   (C) is heavily biased against American policy

   (D) is always completely accurate

STOP

How Am I Doing?

Mini-Test 1

Page 88

Number Correct

6 answers correct	**Great Job!** Move on to the section test on page 108.
4–5 answers correct	**You're almost there!** But you still need a little practice. Review practice pages 81–87 before moving on to the section test on page 108.
0–3 answers correct	**Oops!** Time to review what you have learned and try again. Review the practice section on pages 81–87. Then, retake the test on page 88. Now, move on to the section test on page 108.

Mini-Test 2

Page 93

Number Correct

2 answers correct	**Awesome!** Move on to the section test on page 108.
1 answer correct	**You're almost there!** But you still need a little practice. Review practice pages 89–92 before moving on to the section test on page 108.
0 answers correct	**Oops!** Time to review what you have learned and try again. Review the practice section on pages 89–92. Then, retake the test on page 93. Now, move on to the section test on page 108.

Mini-Test 3

Page 100

Number Correct

8 answers correct	**Great Job!** Move on to the section test on page 108.
5–7 answers correct	**You're almost there!** But you still need a little practice. Review practice pages 94–99 before moving on to the section test on page 108.
0–4 answers correct	**Oops!** Time to review what you have learned and try again. Review the practice section on pages 94–99. Then, retake the test on page 100. Now, move on to the section test on page 108.

How Am I Doing?

Mini-Test 4	7 answers correct	**Awesome!** Move on to the section test on page 108.
Page 105 **Number Correct**	5–6 answers correct	**You're almost there!** But you still need a little practice. Review practice pages 101–104 before moving on to the section test on page 108.
	0–4 answers correct	**Oops!** Time to review what you have learned and try again. Review the practice section on pages 101–104. Then, retake the test on page 105. Now, move on to the section test on page 108.

Final Social Studies Test
for pages 81–104

DIRECTIONS: The following excerpts from *The New England Primer* were used to teach colonial American children the alphabet. Use them to answer questions 1 and 2.

In **Adam's** Fall We sinned all. Thy Life to mend, This **Book** attend The **Cat** doth play, And after slay. A **Dog** will bite A Thief at night. The **Eagle's** flight Is out of sight. The idle **Fool** Is whipt at school.	As runs the **Glass,** Man's Life doth pass. My Book and **Heart,** Shall never part. **Job** feels the rod, Yet blesses God. Our **Kings** the good, No man of blood. The **Lion** bold, The Lamb doth hold. The **Moon** gives light, In time of Night.	**Nightingales** sing, In time of Spring. The royal **Oak,** It was the tree, That sav'd His Royal Majesty. **Peter** denies His Lord, and cries. **Queen** Esther comes, In Royal State, To save the Jews From dismal fate. **Rachel** doth mourn, For her First-born. **Samuel** anoints, Whom God appoints	**Time** cuts down all, Both great and small **Uriah's** beauteous wife, Made David seek his life. **Whales** in the sea, God's voice obey. **Xerxes** the Great did die, And so must you and I. **Youth** forward slips, Death soonest nips. **Zaccheus** he, Did climb the Tree, His Lord to see

1. **One verse reads, "Thy life to mend/This Book attend." Based on what you know about the *Primer* and colonial American society, "this Book" probably refers to _____ .**

   Ⓐ *The Works of William Shakespeare*

   Ⓑ the Bible

   Ⓒ *Poor Richard's Almanac*

   Ⓓ *The Collected Works of Thomas Jefferson*

2. **Based on these verses, which of the following was highly valued in colonial American society?**

   Ⓕ hard work

   Ⓖ religious faith

   Ⓗ literacy

   Ⓙ all of the above

DIRECTIONS: Choose the best answer.

3. **What is the name of New Zealand's native peoples?**

   Ⓐ Aborigines

   Ⓑ Hawaiki

   Ⓒ Maori

   Ⓓ Oceanians

4. **The Basque language is spoken primarily in _____ .**

   Ⓕ the British Isles

   Ⓖ Spain

   Ⓗ Italy

   Ⓙ Germany

GO

Name _____   Date _____

DIRECTIONS: Use the passage below to answer questions 5 and 6.

It is commonly believed that slavery was the sole cause of the U.S. Civil War. However, historians have held that slavery was simply a symptom of the economic disparity between the North and South, which was the larger cause. It is clear that the South's economy focused on agriculture, while the North was racing along with an eye on industrialization. This difference certainly could have contributed to the outbreak of civil war, but it is not likely to have been the sole cause, in the view of most experts.

Some historians believe that political action was an equally important cause of the Civil War. Their theory states that political candidates seeking election used the issue of slavery to stir up political sentiment and catapult themselves into office.

In the final analysis, most historians agree that not only slavery, but also, on a deeper level, the issues that led to differences of opinion about slavery, caused the Civil War.

5. **Why do some historians believe that politics was one reason behind the Civil War?**
   - (A) Political candidates seeking election used the issue of slavery to stir up political turmoil in the hope of being elected.
   - (B) Industrialists in the North had more money to contribute to political campaigns than Southern plantation owners.
   - (C) Slaves threatened not to vote for candidates who did not oppose slavery.
   - (D) People in the North tended to vote in large numbers; people in the South did not.

6. **This passage demonstrates that _____ .**
   - (F) you can always trust what you read in history books
   - (G) most American history textbooks are unreliable
   - (H) historians sometimes disagree about the reasons behind events
   - (J) all opinions about historical events have equal validity

DIRECTIONS: Choose the best answer.

7. **Japan is an example of a(n) _____ .**
   - (A) isthmus
   - (B) peninsula
   - (C) strait
   - (D) archipelago

8. **Which of the following states is located east of the Mississippi River?**
   - (F) Oklahoma
   - (G) Illinois
   - (H) Missouri
   - (J) Kansas

9. **Which of the following practices would likely cause the greatest tension between the people who practice a religion and the government?**
   - (A) marrying more than one person at a time
   - (B) discouraging women from cutting their hair
   - (C) praying five times daily
   - (D) refusing to eat pork products

10. **Presidential elections are held during _____ .**
    - (F) April
    - (G) January
    - (H) November
    - (J) December

11. **A rate of increase in the general price level of all goods and services is called _____ .**
    - (A) a tariff
    - (B) a subsidy
    - (C) supply and demand
    - (D) inflation

GO

12. To be accepted as part of the Constitution, a proposed amendment must be ratified by what fraction of the states?

(F) one-third

(G) three-fourths

(H) two-thirds

(J) over fifty percent

13. A maximum wage _____ .

(A) is the lowest legal wage a worker can be paid

(B) is a limit on how much income an individual can earn

(C) is most likely to be supported by top executives

(D) primarily hurts low-paid workers

14. The gross domestic product _____ .

(F) measures the average change over time in the prices of commonly used goods and services

(G) is a payment by a government to the producer of a good or service

(H) is the total value of goods and services produced by a nation

(J) is a tax charged on imported goods.

15. Creating an identical genetic copy of an original cell or organism is called _____ .

(A) cloning

(B) genetic modification

(C) gene enhancement

(D) duplication

DIRECTIONS: Use the table in the next column to answer questions 16 and 17.

12 Largest Ancestries in the U.S. (2000)

The Census Bureau defines ancestry as a person's ethnic origin, heritage, descent, or "roots," which may reflect their place of birth, place of birth of parents or ancestors, and ethnic identities that have evolved within the United States.

Ancestry	Number	Percent of Total U.S. Population
German	42,841,569	15.2
Irish	30,524,799	10.8
African American	24,903,412	8.8
English	24,509,692	8.7
Mexican	18,382,291	6.5
Italian	15,638,348	5.6
Polish	8,977,235	3.2
French	8,309,666	3.0
American Indian	7,876,568	2.8
Scottish	4,890,581	1.7
Dutch	4,541,770	1.6
Norwegian	4,477,725	1.6

Source: U.S. Census Bureau

16. More Americans identify themselves as having this ancestry than any other.

(F) African-American

(G) German

(H) Scottish

(J) American Indian

17. What can you conclude from the information in the table?

(A) There are more African Americans in the United States than any other ethnic group.

(B) Most Americans have ancestors from English-speaking countries.

(C) The majority of Americans are of European ancestry.

(D) Ancestry is unimportant to most Americans.

STOP

Name _____ Date _____

Final Social Studies Test
Answer Sheet

1. Ⓐ Ⓑ Ⓒ Ⓓ
2. Ⓕ Ⓖ Ⓗ Ⓙ
3. Ⓐ Ⓑ Ⓒ Ⓓ
4. Ⓕ Ⓖ Ⓗ Ⓙ
5. Ⓐ Ⓑ Ⓒ Ⓓ
6. Ⓕ Ⓖ Ⓗ Ⓙ
7. Ⓐ Ⓑ Ⓒ Ⓓ
8. Ⓕ Ⓖ Ⓗ Ⓙ
9. Ⓐ Ⓑ Ⓒ Ⓓ
10. Ⓕ Ⓖ Ⓗ Ⓙ

11. Ⓐ Ⓑ Ⓒ Ⓓ
12. Ⓕ Ⓖ Ⓗ Ⓙ
13. Ⓐ Ⓑ Ⓒ Ⓓ
14. Ⓕ Ⓖ Ⓗ Ⓙ
15. Ⓐ Ⓑ Ⓒ Ⓓ
16. Ⓕ Ⓖ Ⓗ Ⓙ
17. Ⓐ Ⓑ Ⓒ Ⓓ

Science Standards

Standard 1—Unifying Concepts and Processes *(See pages 114–115.)*
As a result of the activities in grades K–12, all students should develop understanding and abilities aligned with the following concepts and processes:
- Systems, order, and organization.
- Evidence, models, and explanation.
- Constancy, change, and measurement.
- Evolution and equilibrium.
- Form and function.

Standard 2—Science as Inquiry *(See pages 116–117.)*
As a result of their activities in grades 5–8, all students should develop
- Abilities necessary to do scientific inquiry.
- Understandings about scientific inquiry.

Standard 3—Physical Science *(See pages 119–121.)*
As a result of their activities in grades 5–8, all students should develop an understanding of
- Properties and changes of properties in matter.
- Motion and forces.
- Transfer of energy.

Standard 4—Life Science *(See pages 122–124.)*
As a result of their activities in grades 5–8, all students should develop an understanding of
- Structure and function in living systems.
- Reproduction and heredity.
- Regulation and behavior.
- Populations and ecosystems.
- Diversity and adaptations of organisms.

Standard 5—Earth and Space Science *(See pages 125–126.)*
As a result of their activities in grades 5–8, all students should develop an understanding of
- Structure of the Earth system.
- Earth's history.
- Earth in the solar system.

Standard 6—Science and Technology *(See page 128.)*
As a result of their activities in grades 5–8, all students should develop
- Abilities of technological design.
- Understandings about science and technology.

Standard 7—Science in Personal and Social Perspectives *(See page 129.)*
As a result of their activities in grades 5–8, all students should develop an understanding of
- Personal health.
- Populations, resources, and environments.
- Natural hazards.
- Risks and benefits.
- Science and technology in society.

Science Standards

Standard 8—History and Nature of Science *(See page 130.)*
As a result of their activities in grades 5–8, all students should develop an understanding of
- Science as a human endeavor.
- Nature of science.
- History of science.

Science

Examining Evidence and Providing Explanations

Unifying Concepts and Processes

DIRECTIONS: Read the passage below, and then answer the questions that follow.

> Some people believe that Earth is not a round sphere but a flat disc that resembles a CD or old phonograph record. According to "flat-earthers," the North Pole is at the center of the disc. A 150-foot-high wall of ice surrounds the disc's edge; nobody has ever crossed this wall. There is no South Pole; what people call the South Pole is actually the wall of ice. The equator is a circle halfway between the North Pole and the wall of ice.
>
> Flat-earthers offer the following evidence and explanations for their belief:
> * Many Biblical passages suggest that Earth is flat.
> * The surface of every body of water is flat.
> * The land looks flat to the naked eye. Even atop a high hill or when measured by surveyors' instruments, Earth looks flat.
> * Nature proves that there is an "up" and a "down." If Earth were round, people in Australia would fall off; there is no gravitation.
> * The circumference of Earth at 45° south latitude is twice what it is at 45° north latitude, because in the south the meridians of longitude spread out as they grow nearer to the wall of ice.
> * The space program is a fraud. The so-called "Moon landings" did not occur; they were filmed in Hollywood and passed off as real to the public.
> * In some lunar eclipses, both the Moon and the sun are visible above the horizon. This proves that Earth cannot be a round body positioned between the sun and the Moon.

 Clue An explanation is scientific if it is observable, natural, consistent, testable, predictable, and tentative (subject to revision and correction).

1. **Is the flat Earth argument scientific? Why or why not? If not, what makes the explanations unscientific?**

   _____

   _____

   _____

   _____

   _____

   _____

   _____

2. **What evidence do you have that the Earth is not flat? Is your evidence scientific? Why or why not?**

   _____

   _____

   _____

   _____

   _____

   _____

   _____

STOP

Name _____   Date _____

Dichotomous Keys
Unifying Concepts and Processes

DIRECTIONS: Obtain samples of the following kinds of snack foods: pretzels, potato chips, buttered popcorn, tortilla chips, corn chips, and caramel popcorn. Use index cards to note the similarities and differences between the different snacks. Then, on a separate page, develop a dichotomous key to identify the snacks.

Clue Scientists use similarities and differences to classify the natural world around them. The tool they use to do this is called the dichotomous key. *Dichotomous* means "two choices." Scientists can use a dichotomous key to identify any object or organism included in the key. Each object or organism fits into one of two choices in the key. As a scientist moves down through the choice steps, eventually the object or organism will be described and identified.

To read a dichotomous key, compare the characteristics of an unknown object against the key. The key will begin with general characteristics and lead to increasingly specific characteristics. By following the key and making the correct choices, you should be able to identify the object.

For example, suppose you found a jar of beans in the kitchen but you don't know what kind of beans they are. You might use the following dichotomous key to identify the beans in the jar.

1a. Bean is round.	**Garbanzo bean**
1b. Bean is elliptical or oblong.	Go to 2
2a. Bean is white.	**White northern bean**
2b. Bean has dark pigments.	Go to 3
3a. Bean is evenly pigmented.	Go to 4
3b. Bean pigmentation is mottled.	**Pinto bean**
4a. Bean is black.	**Black bean**
4b. Bean is reddish-brown.	**Kidney bean**

To make your own dichotomous key, closely examine and write down the characteristics of the objects you are classifying. Start with the most general characteristics and progress to increasingly more specific characteristics. Group together objects that have similar characteristics (for example, similar size, shape, or color). Determine which characteristic gives you the least number of subgroups. This is a good starting point for the key. Then, determine how to break down each subgroup into smaller subgroups, using pairs of characteristics. Keep working until you have identified all of your objects using these subgroups.

STOP

Science
2.0 | Hypothesizing and Experimenting
Science as Inquiry

DIRECTIONS: Read about the experiment below, and then follow the steps to conduct the experiment. Complete the table and graph described in the steps and answer all questions.

In this experiment, you will dissolve an effervescent tablet in three different cups of water: one containing cold water, one hot water, and one at room temperature. You will measure how fast the tablet dissolves in each type of water.

HYPOTHESIZING

Before you begin the experiment, first make a hypothesis about what will happen.

1. **What is the variable in this experiment?**

   _____

   _____

2. **What do you think the relationship will be between the water temperature and the time it takes for the tablet to dissolve? Which tablet will disappear the quickest? the slowest?**

   _____

   _____

   _____

   _____

   _____

   _____

   _____

   _____

   _____

PREPARING FOR THE EXPERIMENT

- Obtain the following items: three 8-oz. cups or jars, three effervescent tablets, a thermometer, a measuring cup, and a watch or clock with a second hand.
- Use whole, not broken, tablets.
- Preheat water to about 160°F (or use hot tap water).
- Have cold and room-temperature water also ready.

CONDUCTING THE EXPERIMENT

3. **Add 1 cup (8-oz.) of the cold water to one of the cups. Measure the water temperature and record it in the table below.**

	Water temperature	Time for tablet to dissolve
Cold water		
Room-temperature water		
Hot water		

GO

4. Consult your watch or clock; as the second hand reaches the 12, drop an effervescent tablet into the cup of cold water.

5. Observe what occurs in the cup. Do not stir the mixture.

6. When the tablet is completely dissolved, consult your watch or clock again. In the table on the previous page, record the time it took for the tablet to dissolve.

7. Repeat steps 3–6 for the room-temperature water and the hot water. Be sure that you make no other changes.

8. In the space below, create a line graph to illustrate the results of your experiment. Plot the time it took each tablet to dissolve on the vertical axis and the water temperature on the horizontal axis.

9. On the lines below, explain how your results compared to your hypothesis.

_____

_____

_____

_____

_____

_____

STOP

Science

| 1.0–2.0 |

For pages 114–117

DIRECTIONS: Choose the best answer.

1. **Which of the following should you do first if you want to set up your own science experiment?**

    (A) Gather the necessary materials.

    (B) Make a hypothesis.

    (C) Evaluate your data.

    (D) Record your data.

2. **Something in an experiment that can change is called a _____ .**

    (F) control

    (G) hypothesis

    (H) variable

    (J) theory

DIRECTIONS: Read the passage below, and then answer questions 3 and 4.

Suppose you own two cats, both of which have developed sores. You think that the type of cat litter you are using is causing the sores. You change the type of cat litter and the type of food one cat receives. You make no changes to the litter and food the other cat uses. Other than the difference in food and litter, you treat both animals the same.

3. **The experiment described above is flawed because _____ .**

    (A) you are using more than one variable

    (B) you are not using enough variables

    (C) the experiment cannot be repeated

    (D) the experiment has no control

4. **One way to make the experiment valid would be to _____ .**

    (F) change the amount of water each cat receives as well

    (G) change only the litter the first cat receives, but not the food

    (H) change neither the litter nor the food the cats receive

    (H) all of the above

DIRECTIONS: Use the dichotomous key below to answer question 5.

1. Larger than 6 inches—go to 2
   Not larger than 6 inches—go to 3

2. Has molars and canines—go to 5
   Has only molars—go to 4

3. Light weight/hollow bones in skull—go to 6
   Heavy/not hollow bones in skull—go to 7

4. Approximately 18 inches—Cow
   Approximately 16 inches—Deer

5. No tusks present—Dog
   Tusks present—Warthog

6. Curved sharp beak—Hawk
   Pointed beak—Sparrow

7. Arrow/triangular shaped skull—go to 9
   Not arrow/triangular shaped skull—go to 8

8. Lower middle incisors long and curved—go to 10
   Lower incisors all same length—Cat

9. Beak-like curved "nose"—Turtle
   Fangs present—Snake

10. Large space between incisors and molars—Muskrat
    No large space between incisors and molars—Rabbit

5. **You are walking in the woods and find the skull of an unknown animal. The skull is shaped like an oval and is $3\frac{1}{2}$ inches long. It has heavy bones and many teeth, including lower incisors that are all the same length. What was this animal?**

_____

Science

3.0

Exploring pH Value
Physical Science

DIRECTIONS: The table below lists some common substances and their pH values. Study the table carefully and think about the properties of each substance. Then, answer the questions on the next page.

Acids and bases in water separate into ions, and the positive ion is hydrogen (H^+). As acids get stronger, the concentration of hydrogen ions is greater. As bases get stronger, the concentration of hydrogen ions is less. The *pH* (potential hydrogen) value of a solution is a measure of the presence of hydrogen ions in the solution. It tells us whether the solution is an acid or a base. In a water solution, acids have a pH value lower than 7; bases have a pH value higher than 7. As acids get stronger, the pH value gets lower; as bases get stronger, the pH value gets higher.

pH	Substance	
14.0	Sodium Hydroxide	
13.0	Lye	
12.5	Bleach	
11.0	Ammonia	**Base**
10.0	Antacids	
10.0	Hand Soap	
8.3	Baking Soda	
7.4	Human Blood	
7.0	Pure Water	**Neutral**
6.6	Milk	
6.0	Urine	
5.0	Coffee	
4.5	Tomato Juice	
3.5	Apple Juice	**Acid**
3.0	Cola	
2.2	Vinegar	
2.0	Lemon Juice	
1.0	Battery Acid	
0	Hydrochloric Acid	

GO

DIRECTIONS: Choose the best answer.

1. **Based on the items in the table, you can conclude that acids are known for tasting _____ .**

   (A) sour

   (B) salty

   (C) bitter

   (D) chewy

2. **Based on the items in the table, you can conclude that bases are known for tasting _____ .**

   (F) sour

   (G) salty

   (H) bitter

   (J) chewy

3. **Based on the table, which of the following is not true of acids?**

   (A) Acids tend to corrode metals.

   (B) Acids produce a stinging feeling.

   (C) Strong acids can cause severe burns.

   (D) Acids are soapy to the touch.

4. **Which of the following is a base?**

   (F) soap

   (G) blood

   (H) bleach

   (J) all of the above

5. **Which of the following do you think would do the best job cleaning a tarnished penny?**

   (A) soapy water

   (B) lemon juice

   (C) milk of magnesia

   (D) baking soda mixed in water

6. **For most freshwater fish, the optimal pH range in the aquarium should be kept between _____ .**

   (F) 1.0–3.0

   (G) 3.0–6.0

   (H) 6.0–9.0

   (J) 9.0–12.0

7. **What do you think the pH value of human tears would be?**

   (A) between 1.0 and 2.0

   (B) about 5.0

   (C) just a little greater than 7.0

   (D) between 10.0 and 11.0

8. **Which of the following has the least concentration of H^+ ions?**

   (F) ammonia

   (G) hand soap

   (H) battery acid

   (J) pure water

DIRECTIONS: Answer the following questions using complete sentences.

9. **Are liquid drain cleaners mostly acids or bases? Give one reason for your answer.**

   _____

   _____

10. **What patterns do you see in the substances in the table? Which substances would be safe to touch? Which would be unsafe? What is the pH range of most foods?**

    _____

    _____

    _____

    _____

    _____

    _____

STOP

Science

3.0

Working with Pendulums
Physical Science

DIRECTIONS: Study the drawing of a pendulum below and then use it to answer the questions that follow.

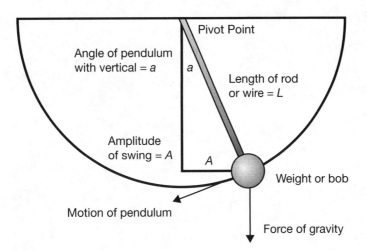

Pivot Point

Angle of pendulum
with vertical = a

a

Length of rod
or wire = L

Amplitude
of swing = A

A

Weight or bob

Motion of pendulum

Force of gravity

Clue

A **pendulum** is a suspended weight that swings back and forth in a regular periodic motion. When the weight is pulled back and released, it swings freely down because of gravity and then out and up because of its **inertia**, or the tendency to stay in motion. One swing of the pendulum over and back is called the **period**. A pendulum's **frequency** is the number of back-and-forth swings in a certain length of time.

1. **When you double the mass of the pendulum bob, _____ .**

   Ⓐ   the pendulum swings twice as fast

   Ⓑ   the pendulum swings half as fast

   Ⓒ   the pendulum's speed stays the same

   Ⓓ   the pendulum will no longer work

2. **If you decrease the length of the pendulum rod, _____ .**

   Ⓕ   the frequency of the pendulum
        is decreased

   Ⓖ   the frequency of the pendulum
        is increased

   Ⓗ   the weight of the bob is increased

   Ⓙ   the weight of the bob is decreased

3. **How does changing *L* affect the period?**

   _____

   _____

4. **How does changing *a* affect the period?**

   _____

   _____

5. **How can you get the shortest period?
   How can you get the longest?**

   _____

   _____

   _____

   _____

STOP

Science

4.0

Populations, Cooperation, and Competition

Life Science

DIRECTIONS: Study the figure below to answer question 1.

1   2   3   4

1. Which of the above figures best represents a population?

- Ⓐ 1
- Ⓑ 2
- Ⓒ 3
- Ⓓ 4

DIRECTIONS: Choose the best answer.

2. When more than two members of a population seek the same resource at the same time _____ .

- Ⓕ competition occurs
- Ⓖ carrying capacity is achieved
- Ⓗ cooperation occurs
- Ⓙ symbiosis occurs

3. Competition for food, living space, and other resources among members of a population most often _____ .

- Ⓐ prevents population growth
- Ⓑ increases population growth
- Ⓒ causes members of that population to cooperate
- Ⓓ benefits all the organisms in an ecosystem

4. In nature, the most intense competition is usually _____ .

- Ⓕ among individuals of different species, because they become innately aggressive toward one another
- Ⓖ among individuals of similar but distinct species, because their needs are so similar
- Ⓗ among individuals of the same species, because they need the same kinds of food and shelter
- Ⓙ a positive thing since it generally increases population growth

5. Which of the following is an example of cooperation in a population?

- Ⓐ An eagle captures and eats a snake.
- Ⓑ Worker ants feed and care for ant larvae that hatch from eggs laid by the queen.
- Ⓒ Two goldfinches want to use the same nesting space to lay eggs.
- Ⓓ A roundworm attaches itself to the inside of a cat's intestine and feeds on nutrients in the cat's blood.

Science

4.0

Basic Structures of Life
Life Science

DIRECTIONS: Choose the best answer.

1. **Which of the following is true of the cells of all organisms, both single-celled and multi-celled?**

   (A) They make up larger organisms.

   (B) They cannot survive alone.

   (C) Each cell has a nucleus that controls the activities in the cell.

   (D) Each cell can digest its own food and replicate itself.

2. **In multi-celled organisms, cells are organized into _____ .**

   (F) organs

   (G) tissues

   (H) systems

   (J) organelles

3. **Which structure in a plant cell is responsible for making food?**

   (A) the nucleus

   (B) the central vacuole

   (C) the chloroplasts

   (D) the lysosome

4. **One way plant cells differ from animal cells is that only plant cells _____ .**

   (F) contain Golgi bodies

   (G) have cell walls

   (H) contain both a nucleus and a nucleolus

   (J) have a cell membrane

5. **Organs are _____ .**

   (A) structures made up of two or more different types of tissues that work together

   (B) groups of similar cells that work together to do one job

   (C) present in every organism

   (D) present only in animals

6. **The leaves and stems of most plants have a green color because _____ .**

   (F) chloroplasts in plant cells contain a green pigment called chlorophyll

   (G) ribosomes in plant cells contain a green pigment called chlorophyll

   (H) the cellular materials stored in the vacuole are usually green

   (J) the cytoplasm in plant cells contains a green pigment

7. **In a dandelion, which of the following is a reproductive organ?**

   (A) flower

   (B) stem

   (C) leaf

   (D) root

8. **Of the following, which is the most advanced level of cellular organization?**

   (F) tissue

   (G) cell

   (H) system

   (J) organ

STOP

Science

4.0

Scientific Classification of Species

Life Science

DIRECTIONS: Read the passage below, and then answer the questions that follow.

In the late 1700s, Swedish scientist Carolus Linnaeus created a system of grouping organisms according to their similarities. The system is based on a simple hierarchy in which organisms are sorted into seven different categories.

A *kingdom* is the first and largest category. Kingdoms are then divided into smaller and smaller groups; the smallest is a *species*. For example, the classification of the bottle-nosed dolphin is

Kingdom	Animalia
Phylum	Chordata
Class	Mammalia
Order	Cetacea
Family	Delphinidae
Genus	*Tursiops*
Species	*Tursiops truncatus*

Linnaeus also developed a naming system, called *binomial nomenclature*, to help scientists name organisms. The first word in each name identifies the organism's genus; the second, its species.

1. **All of the following are true of organisms that belong to the same species except** _____ .
   - (A) they can produce fertile offspring
   - (B) they can reproduce among themselves
   - (C) they all have the same coloring
   - (D) they share similar characteristics

2. **The two-part naming system used to identify various species is called** _____ .
   - (F) binomial nomenclature
   - (G) phylogeny
   - (H) Linnaean nomenclature
   - (J) taxonomy

3. **Scientists refer to the common red maple tree as *Acer rubrum*. The word *Acer* identifies the organism's** _____ .
   - (A) species
   - (B) genus
   - (C) family
   - (D) kingdom

4. **Species names are often dependent on** _____ .
   - (F) what the organism looks like
   - (G) who discovered the organism
   - (H) where the organism is found
   - (J) all of the above

5. **What does *Sequoiadendron giganteum*, the name for a species of sequoia tree, tell you about one of its characteristics?**
   - (A) It is very big.
   - (B) Its leaves are yellowish-green.
   - (C) It has small leaves.
   - (D) It is found only in California.

6. **Which of the following is the closest relative of *Microtus pinetorum*, the woodland vole?**
   - (F) *Mus musculus*
   - (G) *Microtus ochrogaster*
   - (H) *Equus zebra*
   - (J) *Pinus stobus*

STOP

Name _____ Date _____

Science

5.0

Earth's Structure and Plate Tectonics

Earth and Space Science

DIRECTIONS: Read the passage below and study the accompanying map. Then, answer the questions on the next page.

Earth has several separate layers, each with its own composition. The outermost layer of Earth is the *crust*, which consists of the continents and ocean basins. The continental crust is between 35–70 km thick and is made of two layers: a light-colored granite top layer and a more dense basalt rock bottom layer. The oceanic crust is between 5–10 km thick.

The next layer down is the *mantle*, which is composed mainly of silicon, oxygen, iron, and magnesium. It is about 2,900 km thick and is separated into the upper and lower mantle. This is where most of the internal heat of Earth is located. When a volcano erupts, the magma from the top of the mantle reaches the surface as lava.

The most interior layer is the *core*, which is separated into the liquid outer core and the solid inner core. The outer core is 2,300 km thick and the inner core is 1200 km thick. The outer core is composed mainly of a nickel-iron alloy, while the inner core is almost entirely composed of iron. Earth's magnetic field is believed to be controlled by the liquid outer core. The temperature in the core is a tremendous 5,000°C.

Plate tectonic theory says that Earth is further separated into layers based on mechanical properties. The topmost layer is the *lithosphere*, which consists of the crust and solid portion of the upper mantle. The lithosphere is divided into several *plates*, or rigid bodies of rock, that move in relation to each other. The lithosphere drifts atop the hot, molten mantle layer called the *asthenosphere*. This layer allows the solid lithosphere to move around, since the asthenosphere is much weaker than the lithosphere.

Plates meet one another along *plate boundaries*, which are associated with geological events such as earthquakes and the creation of mountains and volcanoes. The map below shows the location of the plate boundaries. Most of Earth's volcanic activity occurs along plate boundaries. Plate tectonic theory explains *continental drift*, the idea that the continents have slowly drifted over the ocean floor until reaching their current positions.

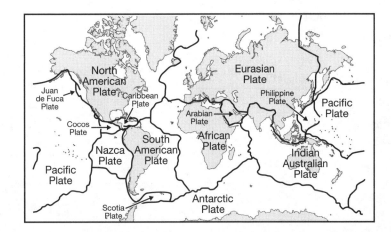

Name _____   Date _____

DIRECTIONS: Choose the best answer.

1. **Earth's core is about _____ km thick.**
   - (A) 1200
   - (B) 2300
   - (C) 2900
   - (D) 3500

2. **The lava that is expelled from a volcano originates in Earth's _____ .**
   - (F) lithosphere
   - (G) mantle
   - (H) outer core
   - (J) inner core

3. **The topmost layer of Earth consists mostly of _____ .**
   - (A) nickel
   - (B) magma
   - (C) iron
   - (D) granite

4. **Which of the following is evidence of continental drift?**
   - (F) Rocks found in Europe matched almost identically to those found in North America.
   - (G) Volcanic activity is rare in Europe.
   - (H) The languages of the world's people all derive from a single, common source.
   - (J) all of the above

5. **Which of the following is the thickest?**
   - (A) the inner core
   - (B) the outer core
   - (C) the crust
   - (D) the mantle

6. **Most of the United States is located on which tectonic plate?**
   - (F) North American plate
   - (G) Caribbean Plate
   - (H) Cocos Plate
   - (J) Juan de Fuca Plate

7. **The map shows that there is a plate boundary _____ .**
   - (A) in the middle of South America
   - (B) in the western portion of California
   - (C) along the New England coast
   - (D) in central Europe

8. **Based on the map, which of the following regions do you suspect has large numbers of earthquakes and volcanic eruptions?**
   - (F) central Canada
   - (G) northern Europe
   - (H) the islands of the Pacific Ocean
   - (J) southern Africa

9. **Matching fossils of land-based dinosaurs have been found in both Africa and South America. In the space below, explain how this supports the theory of continental drift.**

   _____

   _____

   _____

   _____

   _____

   _____

   _____

   _____

Science

| 3.0–5.0 |

For pages 119–126

Mini-Test 2

**Physical Science; Life Science;
Earth and Space Science**

DIRECTIONS: Choose the best answer.

1. **Acids in water separate into ions, and the positive ion is _____ .**
   - (A) hydrogen
   - (B) hydroxide
   - (C) carbon
   - (D) dioxide

2. **As bases get stronger, _____ .**
   - (F) the concentration of hydrogen ions becomes greater
   - (G) the concentration of hydrogen ions remains the same
   - (H) the pH value gets lower
   - (J) the pH value gets higher

3. **Which of the following is a base?**
   - (A) wine
   - (B) lime juice
   - (C) ammonia
   - (D) pure water

4. **The number of back and forth swings a pendulum makes in a certain length of time is called _____ .**
   - (F) period
   - (G) frequency
   - (H) bob
   - (J) pivot

5. **A group of similar cells that works together to do one job is called a(n) _____ .**
   - (A) organ
   - (B) system
   - (C) tissue
   - (D) organism

6. **Three hungry dogs all want the same piece of meat to eat. The most likely scenario in this situation is that _____ .**
   - (F) none of the dogs will get the food
   - (G) all three dogs will cooperate so that each one can have something to eat
   - (H) the dogs will compete amongst themselves for the meat
   - (J) two of the dogs will drive off the other dog, then share the meat together

7. **Scientists refer to the bottle-nosed dolphin as *Tursiops truncatus*. The name *truncatus* is the dolphin's _____ .**
   - (A) kingdom
   - (B) genus
   - (C) phylum
   - (D) species

8. **The oceanic crust is _____ km thick.**
   - (F) 1,000–1,500
   - (G) 120–350
   - (H) 35–70
   - (J) 5–10

9. **The lithosphere drifts atop a hot, molten mantle layer called the _____ .**
   - (A) asthenosphere
   - (B) crust
   - (C) inner core
   - (D) atmosphere

10. **Why does a pendulum continue to move without stopping or slowing down once it is set in motion?**

   _____

   _____

   STOP

Science

6.0

Evaluating Technological Design

Science and Technology

DIRECTIONS: The drawings and text below are from U.S. Patent 11942, given to Dr. Alpheus Myers in 1854. Examine the drawings and text, and then answer the questions that follow to evaluate the design of Dr. Myers's device.

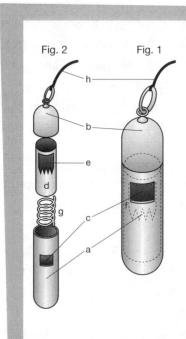

Be it known that I, Alpheus Myers, M.D. of Logansport, in the county of Cass and State of Indiana, have invented a new and useful Trap for Removing Tapeworms from the Stomach and Intestines; and I do hereby declare that the following is a full, clear, and exact description of the same, reference being had to the accompanying drawings, forming part of this specification.

The object of my invention is to effect the removal of worms from the system, without employing medicines, and thereby causing much injury.

My invention consists in a trap which is baited, attached to a string, and swallowed by the patient after a fast of suitable duration to make the worm hungry. The worm seizes the bait, and its head is caught in the trap, which is then withdrawn from the patient's stomach by the string which has been left hanging from the mouth, dragging after it the whole length of tire worm.

1. **In your own words, describe how the device is intended to be used.**

_____

_____

_____

_____

2. **Do you think the device would be easy or difficult to use? Why?**

_____

_____

_____

_____

3. **What potential problems do you think might occur if the device is used?**

_____

_____

_____

_____

4. **Do you think that it is likely that the device would be successful? Explain your answer.**

_____

_____

_____

_____

Science

7.0

Risks and Benefits of Surgery

Science in Personal and Social Perspectives

DIRECTIONS: Read the passage below, and then answer the questions that follow.

Laser eye surgery (LASIK surgery) is a surgical procedure intended to improve a person's vision. Over 1 million people in the United States undergo the LASIK procedure each year. The great majority of patients find the procedure to be beneficial. Successful surgery can eliminate or reduce the need to wear glasses or contact lenses. (Most patients achieve 20/40 vision or greater.) This permits many people to enjoy a wider variety of work and leisure activities.

As with any surgical procedure, however, there are some potential risks associated with laser eye surgery. The U.S. Food and Drug Administration reports that the complication rate of LASIK surgery is between 1 and 5 percent. Possible risks include infection, scarring, permanently dry eyes, light sensitivity, glare, halos, or double vision. A few patients even lose their vision entirely. As a result, individuals considering laser eye surgery should carefully weigh all of the potential benefits and risks before submitting to the procedure.

1. **How many Americans undergo laser eye surgery every year? Of that number, how many develop complications?**

    _____

    _____

    _____

2. **What is the greatest benefit of laser eye surgery? What do you think is the biggest risk?**

    _____

    _____

    _____

3. **What is the name of the federal agency that oversees the safety of laser eye surgery procedures?**

    _____

    _____

    _____

4. **After reading the passage, do you believe laser eye surgery is generally safe? Explain.**

    _____

    _____

    _____

    _____

5. **If you had poor eyesight, would you consider having the procedure done? What steps would you take before deciding to have the procedure done?**

    _____

    _____

    _____

    _____

    _____

    _____

    _____

    _____

STOP

Science

8.0

Science vs. Non-Science

History and Nature of Science

DIRECTIONS: Place an **X** beside each statement below that is not a scientific statement.

Clue

Remember that an idea is **scientific** if it is observable, natural, consistent, testable, predictable, and tentative. **Non-scientific** ideas may be logical and based on good reasoning, but they cannot be considered scientific if they do not meet these criteria. Examples include religious or philosophical beliefs or personal opinions. **Pseudoscience** is an idea that is presented as a legitimate science by its supporters but does not follow the scientific method. Astrology is a good example of pseudoscience.

_____ 1. Green plants will grow toward the sun.

_____ 2. Breaking a mirror will cause bad luck.

_____ 3. Some plants eat meat.

_____ 4. Creatures from other planets have visited Earth.

_____ 5. After Atlas was forced to carry the world on his shoulders, Orion began to pursue his seven daughters, called the Pleiades. Zeus transformed them into stars, and Orion still chases them across the night sky.

_____ 6. Earth has one moon; Mars has two moons.

_____ 7. Lead is more dense than cotton.

_____ 8. If you are a Leo, you are optimistic, creative, and generous. You will be most compatible with an Aries or Sagittarius.

_____ 9. The Bermuda Triangle causes ships and planes to sink and disappear.

_____ 10. The area commonly known as the Bermuda Triangle is located off the southeastern Atlantic coast of the United States.

_____ 11. We know that the world began about 6,000 years ago, and nothing will change that.

_____ 12. The number of human chromosomes was once thought to be 48, but is now considered to be 46.

_____ 13. The African elephant is the largest land animal on earth.

DIRECTIONS: Answer the question below using complete sentences.

14. If a statement is non-scientific, is it untrue? Explain.

_____

_____

_____

_____

_____

STOP

Science

| 6.0–8.0 |

For pages 128–130

Mini-Test 3

Science and Technology; Science in Personal and
Social Perspectives; History and Nature of Science

DIRECTIONS: Choose the best answer.

1. **To be considered scientific, an idea must be all of the following except _____ .**
   - (A) observable
   - (B) testable
   - (C) predictable
   - (D) irrefutable

2. **Which of the following is not a scientific statement?**
   - (F) Saturn is the sixth planet from the sun.
   - (G) Mercury is the eighth largest planet.
   - (H) Venus is the closest planet to Earth.
   - (J) Observing the stars and planets can help you predict the future.

3. **Which of the following statements about LASIK surgery is true?**
   - (A) It has many benefits and no risks.
   - (B) It has some risks, but a person's vision is always improved.
   - (C) It has some risks, but many people consider the potential benefits worth the risks.
   - (D) It can improve a person's vision, but most people still need glasses or contact lenses.

4. **Suppose that you are a store manager who is considering whether to sell a new invention. List two questions that you could ask to help you evaluate the design of the invention.**

   _____

   _____

   _____

   _____

DIRECTIONS: Read the passage below and then answer question 5.

At the time of the American Revolution, about 95 percent of American workers were engaged in agriculture. By 1900, technological advances had greatly reduced that percentage; still, more than $\frac{1}{3}$ of all American laborers were farmers. Today, barely 1 percent of American workers are farmers. The rapid decrease in the number of farmers needed to produce the nation's food has caused great migrations of people out of rural communities, resulting in the virtual disappearance of what was only recently the predominant way of life in America. A 1998 USDA report on family farming commented on the "greater concentration of assets and wealth in fewer and larger farms and fewer and larger agribusiness firms."

5. **What has been gained by the technological advances in agriculture? Has anything been lost? Do the benefits outweigh the losses? Explain your views.**

   _____

   _____

   _____

   _____

   _____

   _____

   _____

   _____

   _____

   _____

   _____

   STOP

How Am I Doing?

Mini-Test 1

Page 118

Number Correct

5 answers correct	**Great Job!** Move on to the section test on page 133.
4 answers correct	**You're almost there!** But you still need a little practice. Review practice pages 114–117 before moving on to the section test on page 133.
0–3 answers correct	**Oops!** Time to review what you have learned and try again. Review the practice section on pages 114–117. Then, retake the test on page 118. Now, move on to the section test on page 133.

Mini-Test 2

Page 127

Number Correct

9–10 answers correct	**Awesome!** Move on to the section test on page 133.
6–8 answers correct	**You're almost there!** But you still need a little practice. Review practice pages 119–126 before moving on to the section test on page 133.
0–5 answers correct	**Oops!** Time to review what you have learned and try again. Review the practice section on pages 119–126. Then, retake the test on page 127. Now, move on to the section test on page 133.

Mini-Test 3

Page 131

Number Correct

5 answers correct	**Great Job!** Move on to the section test on page 133.
4 answers correct	**You're almost there!** But you still need a little practice. Review practice pages 128–130 before moving on to the section test on page 133.
0–3 answers correct	**Oops!** Time to review what you have learned and try again. Review the practice section on pages 128–130. Then, retake the test on page 131. Now, move on to the section test on page 133.

Final Science Test
for pages 114–130

DIRECTIONS: Study the table below and then answer question 1.

Day of week	High temperature
Sunday	26°C
Monday	24°C
Tuesday	84°F
Wednesday	24°C
Thursday	81°F
Friday	79°F
Saturday	26°C
Average high temperature	**49.14°**

1. **You want to determine the average high temperature for the week in your town. You organize your findings in the above table. What data collection error have you made?**

   (A) You have not measured the temperature on enough days.

   (B) You should have measured the low temperature on each day also, for comparison's sake.

   (C) You have used two different systems to measure the temperature; you should have used only one of these.

   (D) You did not need to measure the temperature on the weekend.

DIRECTIONS: Choose the best answer.

2. **To avoid making an error, a scientist should never _____ .**

   (F) record observations from memory rather than as they happen

   (G) make estimates rather than count every individual in a large population

   (H) use samples rather than observe every individual in a large population

   (J) all of the above

3. **Which of the following is a reason to be skeptical of a claim someone makes in the name of science?**

   (A) The claim was observed through a telescope and not by the naked eye.

   (B) The claim is not offered as authoritative truth, but is instead only tentatively offered.

   (C) No other scientist has been able to repeat it.

   (D) The claim is repeatable.

4. **You conduct an experiment to determine whether a celery stalk absorbs food coloring in salty water more quickly than in non-salty water. You put two drops of food coloring plus some salt in one glass of water. You put one drop of food coloring and no salt in the other glass. Then, you put a celery stalk in each glass. What is the error in this experiment?**

   (F) Two different pieces of celery are being used.

   (G) The experiment contains only one variable.

   (H) The experiment contains more than one variable.

   (J) Not enough food coloring is being used.

GO

5. **Which of the following would not be an appropriate step in a dichotomous key to identify a plant?**

   (A) The plant has simple leaves.
   The plant has compound leaves.

   (B) The leaf margins are serrated.
   The leaf margins are entire.

   (C) The leaves are alternate.
   The leaves are opposite.

   (D) The plant has flowers.
   The plant does not have flowers.

6. **As acids get stronger, _____ .**

   (F) the concentration of hydrogen ions becomes less

   (G) the concentration of hydrogen ions remains the same

   (H) the pH value gets lower

   (J) the pH value gets higher

7. **Organs are further organized into _____ .**

   (A) cells

   (B) tissues

   (C) systems

   (D) organelles

8. **Competition between species for resources is reduced in ecosystems _____ .**

   (F) that contain predators

   (G) that consist entirely of herbivores

   (H) with scarce resources

   (J) with many individuals of similar species

9. **Which of the following describes a way animals cooperate with each other to protect themselves from predators?**

   (A) A white-tailed deer that detects the presence of wolves will alert the other deer in the herd.

   (B) Moose are so large that few predators will attack them.

   (C) Porcupines have sharp quills that prevent most predators from eating them.

   (D) Chameleons can change color to blend in with their surroundings and hide from predators.

10. **Which of the following is a scientific statement?**

    (F) UFOs have been observed by many people.

    (G) Flying saucers containing extraterrestrial visitors from another planet exist.

    (H) People who believe in life on other planets are funny.

    (J) none of the above

11. **One way to be sure that an idea is scientific is if _____ .**

    (A) someone with a science degree verifies that the idea is scientific

    (B) it is taught in an American college or university

    (C) lots of smart people believe it

    (D) it is consistent, testable, and predictable

12. **In the scientific name, *Eucalyptus globulus*, the word *Eucalyptus* identifies the organism's _____ .**

    (F) species

    (G) genus

    (H) family

    (J) order

GO

13. Which of the following is base?

- (A) milk
- (B) baking soda
- (C) coffee
- (D) cola

14. One swing of a pendulum over and back is called the _____ .

- (F) period
- (G) frequency
- (H) amplitude
- (J) angle

15. When the weight of a pendulum is pulled back and released, it swings freely down because of _____ .

- (A) gravity
- (B) inertia
- (C) friction
- (D) magnetism

16. Which of the following is the most basic unit in organisms?

- (F) tissue
- (G) cell
- (H) system
- (J) organ

DIRECTIONS: Study the diagram on the right to answer questions 17–20.

17. Which of the elements identified in the diagram is divided into several tectonic plates?

- (A) 1
- (B) 2
- (C) 5
- (D) 6

18. Element 5 in the diagram identifies the _____ .

- (F) lithosphere
- (G) asthenosphere
- (H) inner core
- (J) outer core

19. What is the composition of element 6 in the diagram?

- (A) granite and basalt rock
- (B) almost entirely iron
- (C) silicon, oxygen, iron, and magnesium
- (D) a nickel-iron alloy

20. When a volcano erupts, the magma comes from element _____ .

- (F) 3
- (G) 4
- (H) 5
- (J) 6

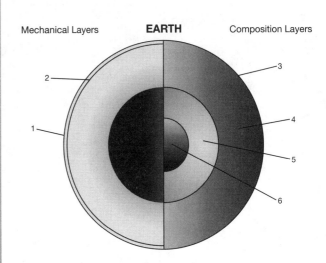

Mechanical Layers   **EARTH**   Composition Layers

STOP

Name _____ Date _____

Final Science Test

Answer Sheet

1 (A) (B) (C) (D)
2 (F) (G) (H) (J)
3 (A) (B) (C) (D)
4 (F) (G) (H) (J)
5 (A) (B) (C) (D)
6 (F) (G) (H) (J)
7 (A) (B) (C) (D)
8 (F) (G) (H) (J)
9 (A) (B) (C) (D)
10 (F) (G) (H) (J)

11 (A) (B) (C) (D)
12 (F) (G) (H) (J)
13 (A) (B) (C) (D)
14 (F) (G) (H) (J)
15 (A) (B) (C) (D)
16 (F) (G) (H) (J)
17 (A) (B) (C) (D)
18 (F) (G) (H) (J)
19 (A) (B) (C) (D)
20 (F) (G) (H) (J)

Answer Key

Pages 9–10
1. D
2. F
3. C
4. F
5. B
6. J
7. D
8. G
9. C
10. H

Pages 11–12
1. a school gym
2. The school's mascot is Eagles. The girls yell, "Go, Eagles!" as they perform their cheerleading routines. The school color is probably hunter-green, because all the girls—except Tracy—are wearing that color.
3. She bit her lip, her chest is tight, she moaned, she swallowed hard and felt as if she was going to throw up and faint.
4. Tracy is trying out to become a cheerleader. She is performing in front of judges, as are a number of other girls. From behind the door of the gym, Tracy hears other girls yelling, "Go, Eagles!" She yells this herself after she completes a tumbling run.

5. Tracy's grandmother told her to break problems into little steps. As she waits her turn, Tracy tells herself to take things "one step at a time," echoing her grandmother's advice.
6. "She let her breath out in a long hiss, then took off."
7. On her second tumbling run, she realized she was performing well. She landed the flip and grinned.

Page 13
1. People are known by the company they keep.
2. United we stand, divided we fall.
3. Misery loves company.
4. Persuasion is better than force.

Page 14
1. This is an example of a realistic poem. It is extremely unsentimental.
2. Students' answers will vary but should generally focus on the finality of death.

Page 15
1. C
2. G
3. D
4. J

5. B
6. F
7. A
8. H

Pages 16–17
1. B
2. J
3. A
4. G
5. D
6. F
7. B
8. H
9. ruddier
10. valor
11. recesses
12. offspring
13. argent
14. the morrow
15. foliage
16. vigor
17. weird
18. The passage describes a band of Native Americans (Mohawks). The men have completed the day's hunt. Some of the women are tending the children. One is caring for a newborn baby, whose name is Thayendanegea. The passage says that his mother hoped he would be a "man of valor among the Mohawks" and goes on to say that her desire "was to be more than

realized." This indicates that Thayendanegea will be a great Mohawk leader.

Page 18 Mini-Test 1
1. B
2. H
3. massive
4. solely
5. intensify
6. morale
7. D
8. Students' answers will vary but should focus on the contrast between the maiden's view of the sea and that of the drowning sailor.

Page 19
1. excuse
2. skinny
3. obsessed with
4. innocent
5. aroma
6. sensitive
7. Students' paragraphs will vary, but the first paragraph should use denotative terms, while the second paragraph should use connotative terms.

Page 20
1–5. Students' answers will vary but should include proper nouns.
6. cacti
7. analyses

8. wives
9. criteria
10. echoes
11. half
12. volcano
13. phenomenon
14. nucleus
15. crisis
16. Karen was worried about her mother and father's health.
17. The letter carrier's job requires him to walk several miles each day.
18. Our teacher asked us to interpret the ten poems' symbolic language.

Page 21
1. C
2. J
3. C
4. H
5. B
6. J
7. D
8. H
9. D
10. H
11. A
12. J

Page 22
1–6. Answers will vary. Students' compositions should argue for or against the premise that global warming is a serious problem.

Page 23
Answers will vary. Students should adapt their compositions for a younger audience. Their vocabulary and sentence structures should be simpler.

Page 24
1. D
2. G
3. C

Page 25
1. D
2. J
3. B
4. H
5. A
6. G
7. D
8. G
9. C
10. G
11. A
12. H

Page 26
1. B
2. F
3. C
4. F
5. D
6. H
7. D
8. F

Page 27
1. metaphor
2. hyperbole
3. pun
4. understatement
5. understatement
6. simile
7. metaphor
8. personification
9. pun
10. simile
11. personification
12. simile
13. hyperbole
14. understatement
15–16. Students' responses will vary but should use the specified figures of speech.

Page 28 Mini-Test 2
1. B
2. F
3. D
4. J
5. D
6. F
7. B
8. H

Page 29
1. book
2. encyclopedia article
3. book
4. periodical
5. encyclopedia article
6. periodical
7. book
8. periodical
9. D
10. G

Page 30
1–8. Students' answers will vary.

Page 31
Students' answers will vary, but the chart should be completed for each search engine, including one of the student's choice.

Page 32 Mini-Test 3
1. A
2. J
3. C
4. J
5. Answers will vary, but students should give reasons for their choice.

Page 33
1. thinking of you
2. for your information
3. be seein' you
4. as far as I know

5. by the way
6. in my humble opinion
7–9. Answers will vary.
10–11. Students' e-mails will vary, but the one to the teacher should be more formal and without abbreviations.

Page 34
1–3. Students' responses will vary.

Page 35
Students' responses will vary. They should describe a delicious food so that the reader will believe that the student thinks it tastes terrible.

Page 36 Mini-Test 4
1. B
2. Answers may vary, but students should recognize that a letter to the governor should be more formal and should not contain abbreviations and multiple exclamation points.
3. Answers will vary. Possible response: The language should be more respectful, and the writer should provide evidence to support his or her argument.
4. Answers will vary, but the letter to elected officials should be more formal and contain less emotional language than the e-mail to a friend.

Pages 39–41 Final Language Arts Test

1. C
2. G
3. B
4. F
5. B
6. F
7. B
8. G
9. A
10. F
11. D
12. J
13. B
14. F
15. C
16. F
17. B
18. J
19. C
20. J
21. B

Page 44

1. 10
2. 100
3. 1,000
4. 10,000
5. 100,000
6. 1,000,000
7. The exponent represents the number of zeros.
8. 2,456.9
9. 590
10. 615,892
11. 23.4
12. 68,000
13. 5,349,800
14. 7,640
15. 1,839,426
16. 73,215

Page 45

1. B
2. J
3. C
4. G
5. A
6. H

7. C
8. G
9. A

Page 46

1. B
2. J
3. C
4. G
5. C
6. J
7. B
8. F
9. D
10. H
11. D

Page 47

1. commutative property of multiplication
2. associative property of multiplication
3. distributive property
4. commutative property of addition
5. associative property of addition
6. $4.5x + 3y = 3y + 4.5x$
7. $(a + 17b) + 12c = a + (17b + 12c)$
8. $22x^2 + 55x$

Page 48

1. B
2. J
3. C
4. F
5. One algorithm for converting mixed numbers to fractions is: (1) multiply the whole number and the denominator, (2) add the numerator to the sum to find the new numerator, and (3) place the new numerator over the original denominator. Students' examples will vary. A possible example: To convert $7\frac{1}{3}$ to a fraction, multiply $7 \times 3 = 21$; add the sum to the numerator: $21 + 1 = 22$; and place the new numerator over the original denominator: $\frac{22}{3}$.

Page 49

1. linear
2. nonlinear
3. linear
4. linear
5. nonlinear
6. nonlinear
7. A
8. J
9. B

Pages 50–51

1.

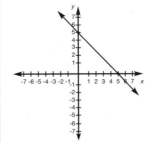

2.

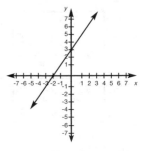

3. The slope of the line is -1.
4. The slope of the line is 0.
5. The slope of the line is $\frac{3}{4}$.
6. question 1: the slope of the line is -1; question 2: the slope of the line is $1\frac{1}{2}$

Page 52

1.

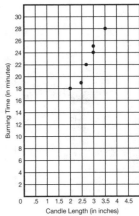

2. $y = 7x + 3$
3. The slope of the line is 7.
4. This indicates that it takes 7 minutes for a candle to burn 1 inch.

Page 53

1.

x	−3	−2	−1	0	1	2	3
y	−7	−4	−1	2	5	8	11

2.

x	−3	−2	−1	0	1	2	3
y	−6	−4	−2	0	2	4	6

3.

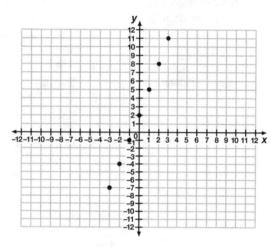

4.

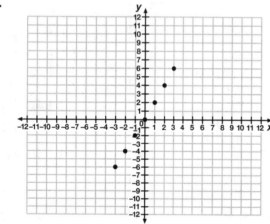

Page 54 Mini-Test 1

1. C
2. J
3. A
4. H
5. B
6. H

7.

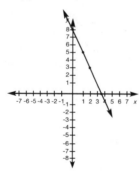

8. The slope of the line is −2.

Page 55

1. According to triangle inequality, the length of any side of a triangle is less than or equal to the sum of the lengths of the other two sides. Therefore, this set of measures can form a triangle because 4 + 9 is greater than 8; 9 + 8 is greater than 4; and 4 + 8 is greater than 9.

2. This set of measures cannot form a triangle because 10 + 7 is less than 18, which violates triangle inequality.

3. Adjacent angles in a parallelogram are supplementary.

4. Opposite sides of a parallelogram are equal in length. In this case, AD = BC and AB = CD.

Page 56

1. Reason: A straight angle measures exactly 180°. If the statements above are true, then: $\angle 1 + \angle 3 = \angle 2 + \angle 3$. If the statements above are true, then: $\angle 1 = \angle 2$.

2. You have proven that the sum of the angles of a triangle is 180 degrees. By following the instructions, you have used the angles of the triangle to form a straight line, which equals 180 degrees.

Page 57

1. B
2. F
3. C
4. G

Page 58

1. $\overline{XY}$
2. $\angle ACB$
3. $\overline{XZ}$
4. $\angle XZY$
5. $\angle CBA$
6. $\overline{CB}$
7. 40
8. 85
9. There are four noncongruent triangles:

Pages 59–60

1. B
2. F
3. C
4. G
5. A
6. J

Page 61

1. B
2. J
3. D
4. J
5. B
6. H
7. B
8. G

Page 62
1. A
2. H
3. B
4. J
5. C
6. F
7. B
8. G
9. km
10. cm
11. m
12. mm
13. cm

Pages 63–64
1. A
2. J
3. A
4. H
5. D
6. G
7. A
8. 340 m
9. 185 cm
10. 3,200 ft^2
11. 200 cm^3
12. 5,086.8 cm^3
13. 137°

Page 65 Mini-Test 2
1. C
2. G
3. B
4. J
5. B
6. F

Page 66

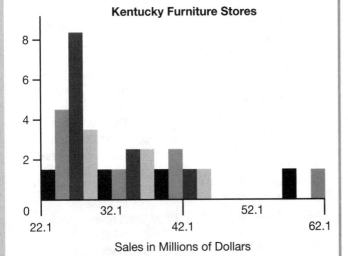

Kentucky Furniture Stores

Sales in Millions of Dollars

Page 67
1. C
2. G
3. A
4. J
5. A
6. J

Page 68
1. From the relative position of the two graphs, students can infer that the hard rubber ball could normally be thrown slightly farther than the soft rubber ball. Students can answer the second question by using the spreads of the data portrayed in the box plots to argue that the soft rubber ball is more variable in the distance it can be thrown than the hard rubber ball.

2.

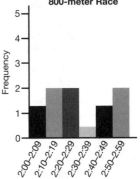

3. The winning high jump height generally increased during the time period covered by the scatterplot. The winning high jump for the 1988 Olympics was probably higher still.

Page 69
1. complementary
2. mutually exclusive
3. complementary
4. complementary
5. mutually exclusive
6. B
7. G
8. D

Page 70
1. B
2. J
3. B
4. F
5. D
6. F
7. C

Page 71
1. B
2. G
3. A
4. J
5. B
6. H
7. D
8. G

Page 72
1. D
2. G
3. B
4. H
5. B
6. G

Page 73
1. C
2. H
3. B
4. G
5. B
6. H
7. B

Page 74 Mini-Test 3
1.

800-meter Race

Frequency

Time (min; sec)

2. B
3. H
4. D
5. G
6. B
7. H

Pages 76–78 Final Mathematics Test

1. D
2. F
3. B
4. H
5. A
6. J
7. C
8. H
9. A
10. H
11. C
12. H
13. A
14. G
15. B
16. H
17. A
18. J
19. B
20. J
21. A
22. F
23. B
24. G

Page 81

1. Aborigines say that ancestral spirits traveled across Australia, made people and left behind the spirits of all those who had yet to be born.
2. The Maori say that a fleet of seven canoes brought their ancestors from Hawaiki to New Zealand.
3. Answers may vary, but students may mention that Aborigines believe in Dreamtime, which connects the land, all living people, and all spirits. They believe such interconnectedness should be held sacred.
4. Answers will vary, but students should mention the Maori belief that all ancestors came from Hawaiki and that all spirits will return there at death.

Page 82

1. Answers will vary but could include religion (numerous references), work/industry (children are to "mind little play"), literacy (children are expected to learn to read), obedience to authority ("parents obey"), and so forth.
2. Answers may vary, but most students should recognize that, because the *Primer* was the book colonial society created to educate its children, the values it taught were representative of society at large.
3. Students' answers will vary, but should include examples.

Page 83

1. Answers will vary, but students should perceive that this passage glosses over the terrible realities of slave life.
2. The passage is not credible, for the reasons students will cite in question 1.
3. Most students should understand that students using this book—particularly white students—likely came away thinking that slavery "wasn't that bad."

Page 84

1. C
2. G
3. B
4. The development of refrigerated railroad cars had the greatest impact on increasing national markets for fruits and vegetables. This allowed produce to be transported long distances and allowed farmers to sell their produce to customers far away.

Page 85

lake (2): *a large body of water surrounded by land on all sides*
isthmus (3): *a narrow strip of land connecting two larger landmasses*
bay (5): *a body of water that is partly enclosed by land; smaller than a gulf*
peninsula (10): *a body of land that is surrounded by water on three sides*
strait (6): *a narrow body of water that connects two larger bodies of water*
cape (7): *a pointed piece of land that sticks out into a sea, ocean, lake, or river*
island (12): *a piece of land that is surrounded by water*
gulf (9): *a part of the ocean that is partly surrounded by land; larger than a bay*
sea (8): *a large body of water that is often connected to an ocean*
archipelago (1): *a group or chain of islands clustered together in a sea or ocean*
ocean (4): *a large body of salt water that surrounds a continent*

Page 86

1. Answers will vary, but students should correctly identify three states west of the Mississippi and three states east of the Mississippi.
2. north
3. California, Oregon, Washington
4. Utah, Idaho, Montana
5. Students can name any two of the following: Minnesota, Wisconsin, Michigan, Illinois, Indiana, Ohio, New York, Pennsylvania.
6. Students can name any three of the following: Texas, Louisiana, Mississippi, Alabama, Florida.
7. west
8. Kentucky

9. Students' sketches will vary but should accurately illustrate their states.

Page 87
1. Slavic family
2. Romance family
3. Celtic and Germanic
4. Both the Romance and Basque families are spoken in Spain.

Page 88 Mini-Test 1
1. Possible answers: Account A says that the attack on the *Maddox* was unprovoked; Account B says that the *Maddox* fired first.

   Account A says that the *Maddox* was in international waters about 30 miles from the North Vietnamese coast; Account B says that the *Maddox* was as close as 4 miles from the North Vietnamese coast.

   Account A says that the *Maddox* was on routine patrol; Account B says that the *Maddox* was providing cover for South Vietnamese attacks on North Vietnam.
2. D
3. G
4. A
5. H
6. B

Page 89
Answers will vary, but students should provide reasons for their answers.

Page 90
Answers will vary, but students should provide reasons for their answers.

Page 91
Answers will vary depending on the ethnic group, gender, and social class of each student.

Page 92
1. C
2. J
3. Answers will vary, but should reflect an understanding of the tension between religious freedom and concern for the welfare of children.

Page 93 Mini-Test 2
1. Answers will vary, but students should explain their choice.
2. Answers will vary, but students should describe a situation that demonstrates a conflict between personal beliefs and institutional expectations.

Page 94
1. D
2. G
3. D
4. G
5. C

Page 95
1. C
2. J
3. B

4. F
5. It is possible for a presidential candidate to win the popular vote and still lose the election, because presidents are elected by majority vote of the electoral college, which may or may not reflect the majority of the popular vote.

Page 96
1. Some people favor minimum wage laws because they argue that a minimum wage reduces low-paid work and distributes wealth more equitably within a society. They also say that a minimum wage puts more money in workers' pockets, which strengthens the economy. Students own arguments will vary, but they should explain their answers.
2. Answers will vary but should reflect an understanding of the possible impact of maximum wages on productivity.

Page 97
1. The largest percentage of workers are in agriculture.
2. Industry makes up the largest percentage of the Chinese GDP, and about 22 percent of the workers have jobs in that sector.
3. Agriculture is the smallest segment of the Chinese GDP.
4. False. The graphs show that industry and service jobs account for about half of the jobs in China, and agricultural jobs account for the other half.
5. Answers will vary but should mention (a) the greater productivity of industrial and services workers than farmers and (b) the contrast between the large percentage of the labor force in agriculture and agriculture's output in the economy.

Page 98
1. The CPI measures the change over time in the prices paid by urban consumers for a "market basket" of goods and services.
2. Students should mention at least two of the following: The CPI affects government payments, such as Social Security; it affects eligibility levels and cost-of-living wage adjustments

for many people; it affects the cost of school lunches; and it is used to adjust the Federal income tax structure.

3. The CPI measures inflation (a rise in prices in an economy) as experienced by consumers in their day-to-day living expenses.

4. The CPI is based on averages; differences noted by individuals may reflect factors associated with specific cities or regions and personal spending choices. In addition, the CPI represents only the spending of people who live in urban areas. It does not measure spending of people living in rural or farm areas or those serving in the armed forces.

Page 99

1–2. Answers will vary, but students should give reasons for their answers.

3. These advances could cause some people to feel that scientists are "playing God" or "tampering" in certain areas. If people begin to believe that genetic engineering threatens their health—not to mention their own individuality—a backlash against science could result.

Page 100 Mini-Test 3
1. D
2. G
3. D
4. G
5. A
6. J
7. B
8. H

Pages 101–102
1. Free trade means that governments remove barriers to trade, i.e., tariffs on imported goods, subsidies for domestically-produced goods, etc.

2. Arguments in support of free trade include the following: Free trade spreads knowledge, expands choices, and increases productivity. It also leads to lower prices, higher employment, and higher standards of living. "Free trade" equals "freedom"— thus free trade is often linked in the public mind to democracy and freedom.

3. Answers may vary. In the 19th century, American businesses said they needed tariffs to help newly established American industries compete with foreign businesses. Taxing imported goods made American goods cheaper, which helped American businesses. Now that American businesses are established and can benefit from cheaper labor abroad, however, they want developing nations to eliminate tariffs so American goods can be sold there cheaply.

4. Many fair-trade supporters believe eliminating tariffs would hinder developing nations' ability to create industries to manufacture goods that are already imported from other industrialized nations.

5–6. Answers will vary, but students should explain their answers.

Page 103
Answers will vary depending on when students complete the activity. Many students may comment on the *New York Post's* rather sensationalist, "tabloid" style of reporting.

Page 104
Tables will vary depending on the current positions of the parties. Students should complete the table in full and then highlight the positions with which they agree.

Page 105 Mini-Test 4
1. C
2. F
3. C
4. G
5. D
6. J
7. B

Pages 108–110 Final Social Studies Test
1. B
2. J
3. C
4. G
5. A
6. H
7. D
8. G
9. A
10. H
11. D
12. G
13. B
14. H
15. A
16. G
17. C

Page 114
1. No, it is pseudoscience. Explanations are unscientific for a variety of reasons. For example, they are not repeatable, ignore evidence, and are not observable.

2. Answers will vary. Students might provide a variety of evidence, such as pictures from space, eclipses, intralongitude distances, and so forth. The evidence is scientific if it

is consistent, observable, predictable, repeatable, tentative, etc.

Page 115

Dichotomous keys will vary. Any characteristic may be used to make each new classification. There are many right answers as long as each division of the key is made according to just one characteristic and states only two choices for each division.

Pages 116–117

1. water temperature
2. Students should hypothesize that increasing the temperature will increase the rate of reaction and the solubility of the tablet. The tablet in the hot water should disappear the quickest while the tablet in the cold water should take the longest to dissolve.
3–7. Students should record the temperature of each cup of water, as well as the time it takes each tablet to dissolve.
8. Graphs may vary, but they should slope down from the upper left to the lower right.

9. Students' answers will vary, depending on their original hypotheses.

Page 118 Mini-Test 1

1. B
2. H
3. A
4. G
5. a cat

Pages 119–120

1. A
2. H
3. D
4. J
5. B
6. H
7. C
8. F
9. Liquid drain cleaners are mostly bases. Possible explanation: Bases do not damage metal pipes like an acid cleaner would.
10. Students' answers may vary. Possible response: Substances become more and more unsafe for humans as they become more acidic or more alkaline. The pH value of most foods is between 2.0 and 7.0.

Page 121

1. C
2. G
3. The shorter the length of the pendulum, the shorter the period will be.

4. The smaller the angle, the shorter the period will be.
5. Shortest: decrease L and a; longest: increase L and a.

Page 122

1. C
2. F
3. A
4. H
5. B

Page 123

1. D
2. G
3. C
4. G
5. A
6. F
7. A
8. H

Page 124

1. C
2. F
3. B
4. J
5. A
6. G

Pages 125–126

1. D
2. G
3. D
4. F
5. D
6. F
7. B
8. H
9. Answers may vary, but students should recognize that there is no way land-based dinosaurs could have crossed the Atlantic Ocean to live in both places. The continents must have been relatively close together at one time.

Page 127 Mini-Test 2

1. A
2. J
3. C
4. G
5. C
6. H
7. D
8. J
9. A
10. According to the law of inertia, a body in motion will continue in motion, unless acted upon by a force.

Page 128

1. The device is a trap for removing tapeworms from the stomach and intestines of infected people.
2. Answers will vary. Possible response: I think the trap would be difficult to use. It would probably be very uncomfortable to swallow, and it would need to remain in the patient's stomach for quite a while, which could be dangerous.
3. Answers will vary. Possible response: The device seems to be a possible choking hazard. It also might cause internal damage as it was being pulled back out of the stomach.
4. Answers will vary. Possible response: The device would probably not be successful.

The idea of a tapeworm being attracted to bait, then pulled out of the stomach, would not work. Tapeworms do not eat food from the stomach; they absorb food predigested by the host. They actually do not even have a mouth.

Page 129
1. About 1 million Americans have laser eye surgery each year. Of that number, between 10,000 to 50,000 (1 to 5 percent) experience complications.
2. Students' responses will vary. Possible answer: Eliminating the need for glasses/contacts is the greatest benefit; losing all eyesight is the greatest risk.
3. the U.S. Food and Drug Administration
4. Overall, the procedure is generally safe. Students' explanations will vary.
5. Possible steps include finding an experienced surgeon, talking to others who have had the procedure, etc.

Page 130
1. [blank]
2. X
3. [blank]
4. X
5. X
6. [blank]
7. [blank]
8. X
9. X
10. [blank]
11. X
12. [blank]
13. [blank]
14. No, if a statement is non-scientific, that does not mean it is untrue. Students' explanations will vary. Possible response: Most people would agree that it is true that we should treat each other kindly, but that is not a scientific idea. Science does not have the answers to all of the questions in the universe or the solutions to all human problems.

Page 131 Mini-Test 3
1. D
2. J
3. C
4. Answers will vary, but questions might take into account the ease or difficulty of use and any problems that might arise when using the invention.
5. Answers will vary, but students should recognize the benefits

of greater agricultural productivity, as well as the loss of a way of life.

Pages 133–135 Final Science Test
1. C
2. F
3. C
4. H
5. D
6. H
7. C
8. F
9. A
10. F
11. D
12. G
13. B
14. F
15. A
16. G
17. A
18. J
19. B
20. G

NOTES

NOTES

NOTES

NOTES

NOTES

NOTES